BLOODAXE CONTEMPOR... ....

Throughout the twentieth century, France has been a dominant force in the development of European culture. It has made essential contributions and advances not just in literature but in all the arts, from the novel to film and philosophy; in drama (Theatre of the Absurd), art (Cubism and Surrealism) and literary theory (Structuralism and Post-Structuralism). These very different art forms and intellectual modes find a dynamic meeting-point in post-war French poetry.

Some French poets are absorbed by the latest developments in philosophy or psychoanalysis. Others explore relations between poetry and painting, between the written word and the visual image. There are some whose poetry is rooted in Catholicism, and others who have remained faithful to Surrealism, and whose poetry is bound to a life of action or political commitment.

Because it shows contemporary French poetry in a broader context, this new series will appeal both to poetry readers and to anyone with an interest in French culture and intellectual life. The books themselves also provide an imaginative and exciting approach to French poets which makes them ideal study texts for schools, colleges and universities.

Each volume is a single, unabridged collection of poems presented in a parallel-text format, with the French text facing an English verse translation by a distinguished expert or poet-translator. The editor of each book is an authority on the particular writer, and in each case the editor's introduction presents not only a critical appreciation of the work and its place in the author's output but also a comprehensive account of its social, intellectual and cultural background.

The series itself has been planned in such a way that the individual volumes will build up into a stimulating and informative introduction to contemporary French poetry, giving readers both an intimate experience of how French poets think and write, and a working overview of what makes poetry important in France.

BLOODAXE CONTEMPORARY FRENCH POETS

Series Editors: Timothy Mathews & Michael Worton

Timothy Mathews is Professor of French at University College London. His books include *Reading Apollinaire: Theories of Poetic Language* (Manchester University Press, 1987 & 1990) and *Literature, Art and the Pursuit of Decay in 20th Century France* (CUP, 2000). He co-edited *Tradition, Translation, Trauma: The Classic and the Modern* (OUP, 2011) with Jan Parker, and co-translated Luce Irigaray's *Prières quotidiennes/Everyday Prayers* (Larose/University of Nottingham Press, 2004) with Irigaray. The first volume in this series, *On the Motion and Immobility of Douve* by Yves Bonnefoy, has an introduction by him.

Michael Worton was Vice-Provost and Fielden Professor of French Language and Literature at University College London. He has published extensively on contemporary French writers, with two books on Michel Tournier, and co-edited *Intertextuality* (1990), *Textuality and Sexuality* (1993), *Women's Writing in Contemporary France* (2003), *National Healths: Gender, Sexuality and Health in a Cross-Cultural Context* (2004), *Liberating Learning* (2010) and *French Studies in and for the 21st Century* (2011). The second volume in the Bloodaxe Contemporary French Poets series, *The Dawn Breakers* by René Char, is introduced and translated by him.

BLOODAXE CONTEMPORARY FRENCH POETS: 3

HENRI MICHAUX

Spaced, Displaced

Déplacements
Dégagements

Translated by
DAVID & HELEN CONSTANTINE

Introduction by
PETER BROOME

BLOODAXE BOOKS

BLOODAXE CONTEMPORARY FRENCH POETS: 3
Henri Michaux: *Spaced, Displaced*

Original French text of *Déplacements Dégagements*
by Henri Michaux © Éditions Gallimard 1985.
English translation © David & Helen Constantine 1992.
Introduction © Peter Broome 1992.

ISBN: 978 1 85224 135 3

This edition published 1992 by
Bloodaxe Books Ltd,
Eastburn,
South Park,
Hexham,
Northumberland NE46 1BS.

www.bloodaxebooks.com
For further information about Bloodaxe titles
please visit our website and join our mailing list
or write to the above address for a catalogue.

Supported using public funding by
**ARTS COUNCIL
ENGLAND**

Bloodaxe Books Ltd and David & Helen Constantine
wish to thank the Ministère de la Culture, Paris,
and the Department of French, the University of Cambridge,
for help given towards translation and production costs.

CONTENTS

Déplacements Dégagements

Spaced, Displaced

GENERAL EDITORS' PREFACE

The Bloodaxe Contemporary French Poets series aims to bring a broad range of post-war French poetry to as wide an English-speaking readership as possible, and it has specific features which are designed to further this aim.

First of all, each volume is devoted to a complete, unabridged work by a poet. This is designed to maintain the coherence of what a poet is trying to achieve in publishing a book of poems. We hope that in this way, the particular sense of a poet working within language will be highlighted. Secondly, each work appears in parallel translation. Finally, each work is prefaced by a substantial essay which gives a critical appreciation of the book of poetry, of its place in its author's work, as well as an account of its social and intellectual context.

In each case, this essay is written by an established critic with a love of French poetry. It aims not only to be informative, but also to respond in a lively and distinctive way to the pleasures and challenges of reading each poet. Similarly, the translators, often poets in their own right, adopt a range of different approaches, and in every case they seek out an English that gives voice to the uniqueness of the French poems.

Each translation in the series is not just faithful to the original, but aims to recreate the poet's voice or its nearest equivalent in another language: each is a translation from French poetry into English poetry. Each essay seeks to make its own statement about how and why we read poetry and think poetry. The work of each poet dovetails with others in the series to produce a living illustration of the importance of poetry in contemporary French culture.

TIMOTHY MATHEWS,
MICHAEL WORTON,
University College London

INTRODUCTION

Henri Michaux was born in Namur, Belgium in 1899, and spent a tense, introverted childhood and adolescence in Putte-Grasheide and Brussels, before signing on as a transatlantic seaman in 1920. His first stirrings as a writer, triggered by the reading of Lautréamont and encouraged by the poet Franz Hellens, editor of the avant-garde review *Le disque vert*, emerged in the early 1920s. But it was not until moving to Paris in 1924 that he responded to more potent waves of artistic exploration, including those of early Surrealism. Major journeys to the Amazon (1927-28) and the Far East (1930-31) were crucial to his future themes of displacement, space and inexhaustible human idiosyncrasy, the contact with India and China, especially, enlarging his awareness of different modes of artistic, psychic and spiritual activity. The later 1930s were marked by further restless travel in Europe and South America, by the increasing flux of painting as a necessary expressive medium, and his editorship of *Hermès*, a review leaning towards deeper psychological and mystical enquiry. After the Occupation, spent partly in the South of France, and the painful accidental death of his wife in 1948, Michaux's work took a spectacular new turn, from 1956 onwards, in a prolonged period of incisive and exciting experiment with mescalin and other drugs. During the same years, his reputation as one of the most disturbing, kinetic and revolutionary painters of the contemporary era extended its influence, as exhibitions all over the world testify. Michaux died in Paris, while never ceasing to uncover the surprises and enigmas of his 'inner space', in 1984.

Spectacle and speed: A crowd come out of the dark

The work of Henri Michaux has always been singularly receptive to the teeming life of darkness, not least the swarms of the subconscious, released to the light and probed in their secret patterns. Hence the title of the first 'movement' of *Spaced, Displaced*, echoing *La nuit remue/ The night moves* (1933): *Une foule sortie de l'ombre/ A crowd come out of the dark*. And, given his intensely 'cinematographic' vision, it is not surprising that it should transport one into that other space, traversed by sharp, accelerated images, which is the cinema.

References to cinema thread their way through Michaux's writ-

ing as a constant corridor of attraction. In the boredom of the journey of *Ecuador* (1929), he speculates on the possibility of sequences of sculptures set alongside the Paris-Versailles railway track which would be animated by the speed of the train, superimposing and fusing their images, a 'plastic cinema' of deformations and hallucinatory movements (see *Ecuador*, p.19). As a traveller in Asia, his appetites are whetted by the theatrical performances of Southern India, a 'spectacle' which, he says, has nothing to learn from cinema, such is its pacy rhythm, frantic concatenation and whip-like energy (*Un barbare en Asie*, p.122); while in Bali the *wayang koelit* or shadow-theatre goes even further, is almost 'meta-cinematographic', in its vibrant projection of the leaping gesticulations of leather cut-out figures on to a screen, infused with a 'strange palpitating, tremulous and electric life' (*Un barbare en Asie*, p.232). And in the postface to *The night moves* (p.204), he speaks of the disconcerting inner projections of the mind, compensatory images for the deprived or ill-adjusted self, saying: 'Such cinema is for one's health', linking it to the mainsprings of his literary work.

From the first moment of *A crowd come out of the dark*, one is aware of a displacement, an abrupt switch to a new context of vision. The eye is taken by surprise, stretched out of bounds, forced to adjust to a reorganisation of visual appearances. This is not the only time that Michaux will refer, directly or indirectly, to his 'virginity of vision reborn, as it were' (*Ecuador*, p.27). And, as so often, the spectacle which commands attention is extraordinarily energetic: joined in mid-movement (with no preliminaries or explanatory transitions), inexhaustibly prolific, surging from hidden sources with no visible means of support. The figures which emerge, like those ill-rooted 'faces' which materialise in Michaux's paintings, do so from the very 'mouth of nothingness', sprouting from the void: so that the finite is transfused by the infinite, the visible by the invisible, and the illuminated and outlined by the opaque and formless. In the process, the superficialities of plot and narration dissolve into insignificance, devoured, as it were, by their own 'beyond': as if the thinness of the signified gave way to, or remained only tentatively imprinted on, a more ambiguous, multiform depth, the spawning matrix of the signifying suddenly brought on stream.

The experience, as in all Michaux's writing, is a turbulent discovery of new signs. In a poem entitled 'Movements', he speaks of 'Signs...not of tunic or roof or palace, not of archive or dictionary of knowledge, but of tortions and violence and jostling, and of kinetic impetus' (*Face aux verrous/ Facing deadlocks*, p.19): not the

servants of a classical order or structured stability, nor part of a storehouse of classified knowledge, but agents of disruption and exploratory departures. It is also an experience of the 'revolutionary': an undoing of the status quo, a revaluation of what constitutes reality and one's relationship with it, a rewriting of its possible equations, and a liberation of its virtualities. So much so that the writer feels himself at 'the crossroads of a new era', as if seeing the world at large, within this mere 'darkroom', on the verge of enlarged, futuristic perspectives.

Michaux's poetry is characterised by its 'evidence': its incontrovertible visual impact; the sense of things, no matter how outlandish or inexplicable, materialising before one's very eyes. This is as true of his imaginary countries, Great Garabagne, the Magic Land and Poddema, the elaborate 'buffer-states' conjured up in *Ailleurs/Elsewhere* (1948), as it is of the present evocations pouring from the screen. And the fact that its spectacle may be an amalgam of fictional representation and mental aberration, does little to diminish the conviction that it is real, that one has touched 'life': life in its most precarious, unstable form (perhaps its only form, if it is to be real life). One symptom is that every physical detail, as if each fraction of reality were intensified to the power of n, is endowed with a quintessential quality. More importantly, the spectator cannot stand apart to contemplate at leisure, but is 'forcibly bound', almost a violated participant, obliged to absorb new rhythms and tempos, new commotions and disturbances, dangerously exposed as his customary defences and brake-powers prove inadequate, and psychic energy is made flesh.

That the crowd surging from the scene should be seen as a band of conspirators is significant. For, by their very presence, they mask their own missing dimension: they are a shifting expression of the undivulged beyond themselves, intermediaries of the inexhaustible secret. Their vertiginous movements, their seemingly human sign-language, occur at the intersection of many things: endless replenishment by means of the void, the absolute eaten by the provisional and eclipsed, total expression combined with holding back, real life with fiction, intense physical presence with the abstraction of the psychic. And the onlooker, in turn, is caught between roles: immersed and detached, threatened and enchanted, connected and disconnected. A living tension to be resolved.

In this respect, his verbal account has its own duality or 'two-faced' nature: its recto and verso, its contrasting or divergent phases, its during and after. For, without a word of warning, the move-

ment may be arrested and forced to change direction, subjected to a different perspective and mode of interpretation. In this case, it is a sharp physical pain which wrenches the 'unworldly' experience back into a more 'realist' framework: the realisation that the effects of a hemianopsia have merged with the spectacle to give it this exceptional animation and foreignness. So the experience is rewritten according to a new formula, by which the poetry and the science, the irrationality and the reason, the magic and the cold light of day, form a different compound. There has already been a problematic encounter between inner and outer reality, mental and physical space, artistic representation and fact. Now, far from becoming sedentary, they redefine the terms of their engagement in the light of a new analysis. In his introduction to *Bras cassé/Broken arm* (1973), Michaux refers to a psychology professor's 'reversing glasses' used in an experiment with students: spectacles showing the world left to right and upside down, which lead to innumerable mistakes and misreadings of 'reality'. *A crowd come out of the dark* in the present volume is just such a dislocation and reorientation of perception, as if the spectacles had been slipped on and off, posing all the problems of assimilation and, finally, rectification. It shows Michaux as the most acute and persevering investigator of vision, contributing uniquely to that enquiry, embracing poets as diverse as André du Bouchet, Philippe Jaccottet and Charles Tomlinson, into the complex interrelations of spectacle and spectator: all the passages and transfers taking place between them, their antagonisms and complicities, the intense and fragile negotiations of the visual and the mental, and the ordinary and the extraordinary.

That a physiological explanation of sorts comes in *A crowd from the dark* after the event to 'put it in place', attributing it to arterial palpitations and so ending the text on a more dispassionate 'scientific' note, does little to minimise the upheaval which has animated, enlarged and enmeshed it. Nor, even if the glimpses of a 'transformed order' have to be relegated wistfully to another day, is the sense of wonder at the exceptional coincidence of factors, the extraordinary 'mixing', which has temporarily overthrown the real in such a superlative way, diminished. In his more exotic journeys to the Amazon, Michaux the disenchanted world-traveller said: 'Here, like everywhere else, 999,999 sights out of 1,000,000 which are a write-off and I don't know what to do with' (*Ecuador*, pp.47-48). Nothing could be further from the truth of the spectacle recounted in the opening chapter of Michaux's book, in the closed dark space of an everyday cinema.

Travel to foreign parts

Voyage qui tient à distance/Journey that keeps at a distance, on the other hand, poses the problem, common to Michaux's work, of travel which does not quite 'gel': journeys where he fails to make the connection or which somehow resist or impede total adhesion. This is as true of his year's journey to the Amazon, hedged with 'No entry' signs and recorded in staccato rebellious fragments in *Ecuador* (1929), where he concludes, 'Now I'm convinced of it. This trip is a blunder...You'll find your truth just as well by gazing for forty-eight hours at any old wall tapestry' (p.126); as it is of his travels in Asia, despite the richness of stimulus emanating from *Un barbare en Asie/A barbarian out East* (1933), where the final message seems to be to leave behind the nagging debate of the world at large and withdraw productively into oneself.

The experience of travel described in *Journey that keeps at a distance* is, compared with the Amazon and Asia, only a micro-journey. But it is characterised from the outset by a singular sense of alienation. The piece is indeed a complex study of the notion of *distance*, not just in the sense of distance as faraway places. It is a journey which is in no way a partnership, having exceeded the limits of the acceptable, and within which he is now an unwilling passenger. Polarised between North and South, oppressive heat and the promise of some vague relief, it is more a limbo and an exile than a sense of direction. And, even on arrival, the feeling of estrangement is no less. Reality is unaccommodating and hostile; known landmarks have been engulfed in a transformation of appearances and the familiar decor has been decomposed. Most importantly, a new *linguistic* suspicion or reserve seems to have intervened since his previous visit, severing connections, inhibiting a commerce which could formerly be taken for granted, and forcing communications to be negotiated on new terms. It is as if the town had *become* a new language: with the same linguistic signs recognisably in place, but affected with a different coefficient and a modified relationship between user and use. There is a further overturning of the traveller's expectations – itself a dislocation of sorts – in that the bed-bound friend who is the object of the visit is on his feet, while he, the mobile one, is drained and simply wants to lie down: as if the poles of personality and situation had been reversed, to the extent that he *disengages* and declines to spend the evening there. Even his hotel room, puritan, parsimonious, goes against the grain, so forcing the subject into further re-arrangements of the balance of

power between inner and outer worlds. Alienation is the *écart*, the unstable dichotomy between self and other. This, rather than any known geographical space, is the territory of the journey.

It is this complex displacement which triggers the feverish adjustments of the mind, elaborated in secret, the messages of which are, in the first instance, incomprehensible. So a second set of enigmatic signs, disturbing his sleep, come to join those of the outside world: irrational alerts to be clarified and tracked down, accompanied by disorientation and vertigo. They find a first focus in the view from one of his bedroom windows of the dark cutting of a street outside and a seemingly derelict house below eye-level: a visual and mental abyss showing again, as with the bottomless cinema screen in *A crowd come out of the dark*, all that the searching eye and the speculative mind can derive from blackness and void. Strange half-and-half world: not only in that the houses stand abandoned between demolition and reconstruction, but that this fragment of street is simultaneously 'other' and a reflection of his mental state, a visible scene and a private metaphor – like him, a piece of wreckage adrift, condemned, vaguely redundant, caught inconclusively between sleep and waking, the animate and the inanimate, departures and destinations.

But the experience has yet to superimpose all its layers. For, spurning this depressing view and opening the window on the other side of the room, the writer encounters a no less extraordinary luminous spectacle: a wide, illuminated avenue, as deserted as the dark street formerly, like a brilliant stage-set awaiting its performance. It becomes, like the other scene, an imperative visionary channel, ravaging (like the 'furrows' of mescalin) the hyper-active eye. One would say that the traveller's room were, to quote the title of a prose-poem by Baudelaire (see *Le spleen de Paris*), a mysterious *chambre double*: a two-lobed apartment of the mind, pulled between opposites, no longer just those of South and North, heat and cold, movement and immobility, but all the enhanced significances of dark and light. As one view was sullen and brooding, so the other is flamboyant and ostentatious, creating a fascinating but over-stretched *chiaroscuro*, suggestive of the disturbing cityscapes of De Chirico, all blinding light and irrational shadow, mute meeting-points of the unreal and the real, abstract and concrete. It is as if the spectacle were a disconnected diptych, of which the traveller is the make-shift hinge: struggling to hold together a double *absurde*, twin irrationalities all the more demanding, intensely 'available', because of their irreducibility.

His movements from one side to the other, like the violent alternations and divergent spasms of mescalin, represent the confrontation of irreconcilables: two times or tempos, two mental and imaginative directions, two orders of perception and implication. They reflect also the shock administered to the real and its normal equilibrium. The poet becomes the battleground of a rift. The rising of the moon over one panel of the scenario adds a further degree of 'alienation', as a fictionalising of appearances and another lurch out of the grasp of the real. It is an unnerving mythical eye, inquisitorial, policing the setting: so creating a duplication of eyes, the moon's and his own, probing in different directions, both disconnected, neither in a contented relationship with what it sees. That the moon's exaggerated presence is described as 'inadmissible', emphasising the difficulty of 'taking it in', serves to crystallise the unassimilable elements at work between these two segments of town excessively at variance, 'colossal ill-matched fragments that I don't know how to deal with'. Such an experience of the 'redundancy' of things touches that of Roquentin in Sartre's *La nausée/Nausea* (1938): where all is *de trop*, and a refractory visible reality offers no purchase to the intellectual grids which seek to integrate and interpret it. Here Michaux is the victim of a conspiracy of unrealities, which come to feed, parasite-like, on his physical weakness and disorientation: as if reality were being denied him, perhaps as a punishment or more permanent condemnation.

Various blocked communications aggravate his difficulty: from having no one to speak to in this alien town, to the over-zealous sound-proofing of the hotel which seals him, dream-like, as if in a glass tomb. Blanks and gaps appearing in the text are themselves a form of alienation: a non-relationship or disconnection of language; while an increasingly fretful, jerky passage culminates in a crisis of exclamations, not attached to anything, which hang unanswered, unreciprocated, as precarious as reality itself.

A break in the writing brings down the curtain on this experience of irresolution and *invraisemblance* (or lack of verisimilitude). It indicates a time-lapse, another gulf of unknown duration, and heralds the restoration of normality. The writer makes his getaway from the town by the first train the following morning, just as in his own Pays de la Magie or Magic Land (also a place of strange signals, disruptive forces and occult interventions) he is summarily ejected at the end (see *Ailleurs*, pp.238-39), so heightening the dichotomy between reality and illusion, the *vraisemblable* and the *invraisemblable*, the assimilable and the unassimilable. The piece

ends, then, with another 'disengagement': a relieved retreat into a re-aligned world, no longer 'out of true', now subdued again by habit and recognisable signs. The subject gratefully resurfaces in the *dehors*, not so much from the fluid nightmares of *l'espace du dedans/the space within* (the title of Michaux's major collective volume, 1966), as from what, in 'L'espace aux ombres'/'Space of shadows', he calls that 'horrible within-without which is true space' (*Face aux verrous*, p.190): a violent intermediary space, unsure of its definition, where one is racked between opposites and pulled to and fro, a restless shuttle doing and undoing relations, stitching and unstitching the self in a whirlwind.

The final sentence, 'The weather, too, was cooler', brings the text firmly back into the matter-of-fact and mundane, putting more distance between us and the preceding explosion of 'unrealities'. More crucially, it makes one aware that some kind of catharsis has taken place, that something in the external world has actually been relieved. It leads one to speculate on the mysterious interplay of energetic mental activities and ambient physical conditions: an example of the potent 'meteorology' of Michaux's world, with its baffling climatic and barometric variabilities; and of his view of poetry as intervention and efficacy, or even a form of magic, whose concentrated psychic force can work changes on the physical world.

Instruments of communication

Musical instruments have long been the intimate accompaniments of poetry, giving it its dual voice, its flight to other dimensions, its most ethereal reverberations: from the poet and his lyre, to Mallarmé's Saint Cecilia (see 'Sainte' in *Poésies*) lightly brushing the harp-strings or 'instrumental plumage' of an angelic wing, to Verlaine's vaguely soluble 'sobbing of autumn violins' (see 'Chanson d'automne' in *Poèmes saturniens*). Michaux's private orchestra is no less closely wedded to his innermost movements, his stresses and obscure aspirations, but his instruments are musical eccentrics, gleaned from dubious sources and enlisted *ad hoc* into the tentative symphonies of his *problème d'être*: surrealistic sounding-boards from a Dalí landscape like the 'violin-giraffe' of '*Le grand violon*'/'*The big violin*' (*Plume*, pp.90-91), violently played through the frets of its enormous neck to the tunnel-like *profundos* of its belly; or primitive pulses like those of his tom-tom, frenetically dissolving the rigidities and interdictions of the world (*Passages*, pp.135-37); or the clanging gong which sets up a

protective wave to shield his cotton-wool interior in 'Je suis gong'/ 'I am gong' (*La nuit remue*, p.188). And through all such manifestations, the instrument is the mirror of his poetry, *is* his poetry. They are a shared identity, and in speaking of the nature and function of one, one is sounding Michaux's poetics as a whole.

Such is the case with *Musique en déroute / Music in disarray*. The instrument in question is of foreign origin, creating an initial *dépaysement* or displacement of cultural association. It has the distance of an outsider. It has no pedigree or credentials, and is almost pocket-sized, lending itself to private rather than public, even furtive performance. Moreover it is defective and has parts missing, deriving its special resonance, like Michaux's poetry, from its *incomplétudes*, from its rough and ready structure or improvised composition. It is no accident that, as epigraph to *Passages* (1950), Michaux quotes a fourteenth-century Japanese writer: 'In the palaces of old, one always left a building incomplete, obligatorily'. Nor that in *Ecuador*, in a piece entitled *Je suis né troué/ I was born holed* (pp.98-101), he writes, 'I have seven or eight senses, among which, that of lack'; and in *Ma vie/ My life*: 'Because of this lack, I aspire to so much. So many things, almost the infinite...' (*La nuit remue*, p.92). Sketched here is a whole aesthetic of 'missing parts'.

It is significant that the instrument in this piece has been cast aside for years, considered unusable, so that the connection of familiarity has been broken. It, too, is an alien object: he and it purposelessly remote, making the 'accident' of their encounter all the more unexpected. He has even forgotten how he came by it: no link of memory bridges the gap. But, as in the best Surrealist images, potent in proportion to the distance of their terms and the electric charge and imaginative leap which suddenly clenches them together, an exceptional conjunction of circumstances is preparing a remarkable fusion. Again, a phase of physical and mental distress, following the immobilisation of an accident, provides the spark: a feeling of uselessness and void, lost dimensions and dwarfed possibilities, which send him looking for an outlet and relief. There is a note of irony that the thing enlisted here for his 'salvation' should be, like himself, broken, out of function: a communication of the deprived, two peg-legs together, so to speak, about to explore in astonishing depth the terms of their affinity. Was it, in fact, the black humour, the resentment and rebelliousness that sent him involuntarily towards this 'marginal', this aesthetically deprived exile or outsider, as a gesture, in order to keep bad company?

The engagement is marked by its instantaneity of response, with-

out forethought or preparation, without fuss or ceremony: art with no finicky preludes, no preliminary airs and graces, reminding one of Michaux's statement that 'the mere intent to compose a poem is enough to kill it'. As in Baudelaire's 'Le flacon'/'The perfume bottle', the most unexpected vitality surges from unpromising appearances, darkness and dereliction. But here a mere sound, rather than a scent, issued from this hollow container, the *sanzas*, unleashes a latent life or *vie antérieure* (also a title from Baudelaire's *Les Fleurs du Mal*). It has its own infinity and vertigo: its life of the abyss. Again one is aware of the surprising triggers which can set the world in motion. In the 'Magic Land' (1941) Michaux's Magi/Magicians sought the secret pressure-points and levers which could move a dead weight. In the preface to *Épreuves, exorcismes/ Trials and exorcisms* (1945), he describes the process of poetic exorcism in these terms: 'In the very heart of the suffering and obsession, one introduces such an exaltation, such a magnificent violence, that the affliction progressively dissolved is replaced by an airy, demoniacal ball'. Here the charge of energy which is to perform the 'exorcism' stems from his acutely frustrated mental state which, dispensing with prudence or deliberate control, harnesses two forces which have never previously seen the need to be enlisted to each other's cause. The reed instrument, for its part, seems to have been lying in wait for such an appropriate brusqueness, irritation and rage, a reminder of all that is born, in Michaux's world, from anger and revolt.

The title of a well-known poem by Michaux is *Contre!/Anti!* (*La nuit remue*, pp.83-84). The sound emitted here is raucous, uncompromising, unillusioned. Like his tom-tom of *Premières impressions/ First impressions* (*Passages*, pp.135-37) which is 'anti-Versailles anti-Chopin anti-alexandrine anti-Rome', it runs counter to the mellifluous, the euphonic and the classical principles of harmonic composition. Its grating, rudimentary repetitions are the voice of the barbarian or vandal, breaking moulds, indifferent to conventions, brutalising complacency and poetry as escapism. Its dissatisfied croak has a pitiless insistence capable of breaking down the hardest state. And, as so often in Michaux's world, this fractious musical exploration reveals itself as a hive of contradictions: not only in its stop-start unpredictability, its high voltage currents and short-circuits (matching those of his own style), which leave it somewhere between musical fullness and deprivation; but in that the thing which seems lame becomes extraordinarily potent, the cramped and diminutive becomes a whole universe, and the resolutely cacophonous forges the deepest harmonic relationship. Indeed, whereas in a poem

such as 'Like a stone in the well' (*Plume*, p.100), Michaux asserts his rebellious isolationism saying 'there are no comrades in negation', here he has found, exceptionally, the perfect 'camarade du "Non"' : two *inadaptés*, two *insuffisances*, ready to enlarge each other's awareness, in which the writer is both explorer and explored, analyst and analysed, musician and keyboard. And, just as in Baudelaire's 'Le cygne'/'The swan', one incongruous, orphaned object becomes the intermediary for a vast, out-reaching communion with the exiles and derelicts of the world, so through this unconsidered, abandoned instrument, Michaux's perception embraces the community of the underprivileged, imprisoned and desolate – so fulfilling in another way his summarising statement from the postface to *The night moves*: 'This experience, which may seem egoistic in origin, I'd venture to say that it is social...so much do its workings seem beneficial to the weak, the sick and ailing, to children, to the oppressed and to misfits of all kinds' (*La nuit remue*, p.205).

In fact, the *sanzas* itself, as he progresses from one infirm reed to another, is a community of rebels: individualistic outlaws not there to blend into some easy harmony or common purpose, but pulling in different directions. Their aim is to waylay, to disrupt, producing an 'art' which remains unfinished and problematical: prone to interruptions and displacements, riddled with lacunae, frustratingly nomadic. It is the perfect (or imperfect) twin of Michaux's own refractory poetry: refusing categorisation, resisting unification, determinedly hostile to art for art's sake, and seeing its essence in action and efficacy. Poetry more likely to break links and problematise by ellipsis than to mould to completion: 'To write, rather, in order to short-circuit', he says in *Face aux verrous* (p.50).

Michaux's text has its own breaks, its disconnections and reconnections: an exploration in stages, pursued in different 'times' and subject to changing states of consciousness. The relationship between poet and instrument is anything but one-dimensional. Coming back to it after a 'cooling-off' period, and dubious that it can have retained its first potency now that they have a 'history' and a degree of familiarity and compliance, he finds an undiminished spirit of resistance, stocked with resources: a refusal of *composition* (both in the artistic sense and in the common French meaning of compromise or collaborationism) and a further breeding of disturbances. As elsewhere in Michaux, one is in the presence of untamed energies, like the invisible flail that lashes against the bars of a cage in the Magic Land or the inexplicable upheavals of the poltergeist evoked at the outset of 'Une voie pour l'insubordination'/'A route towards

insubordination' (1980), or even the irregular spiritual force of the Curé d'Ars, 'blackballed in all his examinations' (*Ecuador*, p.78), whose rare charisma is in proportion to his unacceptability and formal ineptitude – a sign of the poet's affiliation to the odd man out, the black sheep, the eternal trouble-maker, the 'evil genius', whose spirit can be, if not harnessed, then exploited to cause a breach or rift, a destructive discrepancy not easily smoothed over or filled.

This 'music of missing parts', handicapped, even grotesque and always true to its law of deprivation, expresses nevertheless the innumerable hidden voices of poetry: the drama of *force* and *faiblesse*, the obscure tides of engagement and disengagement, the waxing and waning, the resistance to expectation, the stage after stage of surprise. It is an immeasurable anti-word: a sub-language never to be artificialised or systematised, always on the verge, unexpended, in its vibrant, though mutilated, virtuality. One thinks of Nathalie Sarraute's elusive infra-language, circulating between *forme* and *informe* on the underside of clichés and the ready-made (see for example, *Le planétarium, Les fruits d'or* or *Vous les entendez?*); of the dangerous musical energy, synonymous with fracture and un-contained possibilities, which recharges the ending of Marguerite Duras's *Détruire, dit-elle* (Minuit, 1969); or of Roland Barthes' 'rustling of language', always testifying to the impossible expression, and by which 'the tenuous, the confused and the tremulous are heard as the signs of an obliteration of sound' (*Le bruissement de la langue*, Seuil, 1984). And it is finally the throttled *cri* which has the last word, monopolising the text to the exclusion of the author's own commentary: an underground, half-imprisoned yet infinitely 'free' language, still exercising its unsettling, irregular, malevolent and rebellious magic. A study of a *sanzas* which is as near as one can come to a total statement of Michaux's poetry.

Freedom and imprisonment

Michaux's 'spatial consciousness' is one of the most resourceful of twentieth-century poetry: a surprising inheritor of the Baudelairean urge to be 'anywhere out of this world'. The speaker of the poem 'L'insoumis'/'The insubordinate' forever seeks 'new opportunities to lose his footing and desert the odious compartments of the world' (*Plume*, p.70), while the last poem of *The night moves*, apocalyptic in mood, having ploughed its way through a morass of semi-senseless sound-language ('Quand les mahahahas, Les mahahaborras, Les

mahahamaladihahas, Les matratrimatratrihahas, Les hondregorde-
garderies, Les honcucarachoncus, Les hordanoplopais de puru para
puru...'), finally extricates itself, exhausted but purged, in a dream
of space without division or restriction: 'Oh void! Oh space! Unstrat-
ified Space...' (*La nuit remue*, pp.199-200). It is symptomatic that we
see the poet, in a piece entitled 'Entre centre et absence'/'Between
centre and absence', 'meditating at windows, windows with their huge
horizons' (*Plume*, p.25); and that, in his first published work, the future
author of *Ailleurs/Elsewhere* should forewarn, 'Sir is absent, Sir is
always absent, please, bid me farewell, there is nothing here but
imprints' ('Qui je fus'/'Who I was', p.65), and later declare, in a
study devoted to the virtues of ether, 'Me, I'm in love with exits'
(*La nuit remue*, p.69). In that same first collection Michaux records
the 'documentary' case of a certain Benson whose 'soul' slips airily
out of his body as it falls from a New York skyscraper and watches
its shattering collision with the pavements below. And Michaux's
alter ego and protective buffer, Plume, the featherweight anti-hero
of the adventures of *Un certain Plume/A certain Plume* (1930) finds
his distraction and dreaminess thrown incompatibly against the hard
edges and hierarchies of an unyielding world.

Michaux's early extended journeys through South America (1927-
28) and the Far East (1930-31) are the expression of the need for
'breathing space' but, clearly, not its answer. That first feeling of
blocked horizons and claustrophobia registered in Quito, though
perched 2,860 metres in the Andes, is already the proof that phys-
ical travel is a *pis aller*, and that the problem of space, central to
the whole of his work and poetics, will be tackled essentially in the
espace du dedans, with its tortuous itineraries, strange motivating
forces and unexpected forms of locomotion.

The first poem of the section *Où poser la tête?/Where to lay the
head?*, a title suggesting restlessness and an elusive serenity, is
'Paresse': an 'idleness', however, more productive and far-reaching
than the *dolce farniente* and resignation of the eponymous charac-
ter of *Un certain Plume* of 1930. It concerns a contemplative dis-
solution (perhaps an absolution), which has persistently haunted
Michaux's peregrinations, from the final words of *A barbarian out
East* quoted from Buddha, 'Keep on an island to yourself, clinging
to contemplation' (*Un barbare en Asie*, p.239), to his description in
'Survenue de la contemplation'/'Back from contemplation' (*Face à ce
qui se dérobe/Confronting the elusive*, 1975, pp.109-24) of access to
a timeless wordless grandeur, with no intrusions or foreign bodies.
Paresse represents a release, a reinstatement of fluidity and the free-

roaming movements of dream: not dream as Surrealist visual riddles, provocative projections of the tensions of the subconscious, but dream as a virtually weightless state, imageless, without beginning or end, infinitely pliable, in a zone apart from the world and its piecemeal pressures. A 'life in parenthesis' at the other extreme from the author's customary interventions and forcible counter-measures.

Paresse strikes a chord for the whole section: a state, not of re-cumbent rêverie, but of active dream and deepening consciousness, favouring doing and undoing, composition and decomposition, with-out restraint. Its example is reinforced by the mental 'disengage-ment' of 'Plaines où l'on plane'/'Plains in another plane': an app-rehension of space and tranquillity which seems the perfect anti-dote to that 'crisis of dimension' described in *Ecuador* (pp.36-37) as modern man's mortal ailment. Its reference to planes beyond planes emphasises both a multi-layered insulation from the world and the intuition of endless transcendence; while the absorption into a superior 'sameness' (in this case not a palling uniformity but a oneness with no disturbances of self or other) illustrates a different displacement, one described elsewhere by Michaux as 'the only intelligent journey: the abstract' (*Passages*, pp.192-93). So 'abstracted', the poet, like the Baudelaire of *Elévation*, soars beyond the realm of 'sickly exhalations' to know a sense of euphoric flight and purification. But, as with Baudelaire, that incarnation of duality, caught between the 'ecstasy of life and the horror of life', the 'dis-solution and centralisation of the self', Michaux's text succumbs to the laws of alternation and the dictatorship of poles. Earth returns as the encroacher. The finite re-infiltrates. The sense of the 'con-structed' (matched by a syntax of small-scale, fidgety cells) com-bines with the coercion of the linear to re-enclose the text and draw it fatally from the airy to the darkly suffocating. The great wing, like that of the bird seen climbing the vast 'landings of the atmo-sphere' above the Andes in *Ecuador* (p.86) as a visual metaphor of the effects of breathing ether, is forced to land. We have entered an *espace aux ombres* in another sense: space with its own attendant shadows or sombre underside. So, a dialectic is set in place.

The truncated human forms of 'Torso situation' re-awaken other visions in Michaux's work of mutilations, physical abnormalities and monstrosities: those, for instance, of the 'trunk-men' or 'potted manikins' of 'Ici Poddema'/'Poddema calling' (1946), by-products of genetic experiments which call into question human integrity and its very definition. They are also reminiscent of Magritte's severed torsos or De Chirico's sectioned tailors' models, surrealistically ex-

posed in a disquieting intermediary space. One might first assume that these headless bodies are a nightmare of missing parts and 'disconnections', until one discovers that they have found a strange wholeness in mutilation, a completeness by reduction, in that the loss of the head as overseer, with its analytical interceptions and 'know-all' intrusions, has stripped them for a more fundamental awareness, free from distractions, divisions and complicating outcrops, as from the intricate bondage of words. A strange paradox: as if, while endowed with all that diversity of function, they had been in exile; and now, each like a handicapped Buddha described elsewhere by Michaux as having his 'great lips closed to bread and words' (*Plume*, p.110), they have salvaged a semblance of roundness and sufficiency from the extremes of dichotomy and divorce.

Space is again the subject of the title-piece of this chapter *Where to lay one's head?*: space allowed to be purely itself, after the elimination of one's normal, seemingly indispensable habitat. Space as the ultimate intensification of 'missingness', a dematerialisation leaving no trace of even the slightest 'things' of the air: wing, feather or intervening haze. Sky which is uniformly sky, perfectly true to itself and apparently timeless, obliging verbal expression to abandon its superflous embroideries and linguistic variations. But, as the poem progresses, it goes (perhaps inevitably) back: from the apparent serenity of the immense 'clarification' first evoked, to explanatory fragments of its history: so that one looks back to the inner cataclysm, the violent *tabula rasa*, born of intolerable tensions inside the head, which has led to this almost anaesthetised 'spatialisation'. And what appeared to be the securely established 'present' of the poem, the evocation of pure 'sky', is superseded almost imperceptibly by another, perhaps its real present: obstructed with debris and the reminders of stress – as if the whole experience of 'ciel' were deteriorating in the telling; and as if the poem, which started (as do all poems in a sense) from the speechless, can, in its verbal course, only slip further towards loss. Hence its gravitation to the final words: 'a henceforth irretrievable sky'. So, the vicious circle implicit in the question 'Where to lay one's head?' is made apparent, in a poem where space, first offering itself as relief to 'the earthly migraine', then becomes its further aggravator. The poem is caught between the opposites of the same word 'ciel': a Janus sky, opening and closing, moving from infinite access to infinite exclusion. Even its 'timelessness', implicit in the repetition throughout of the one word 'ciel', is, paradoxically, a fickle one, with the word 'désormais' or 'henceforth' revealing the negative face: an eternity of im-

23

possibility and deprivation, against which the text can only throw its finely played gradations of possession and loss.

Other dictatorships are the subject of *Dictées/Dictations*. It is here that one has new glimpses of Michaux's visions of totalitarian regimes and brainwashed states as elaborated in 'Poddema calling'; that one relives his life-and-death struggles against the inflexible overlord he calls 'My King' (*La nuit remue*, pp.13-19); and that the private resistance voice which dug in its heels in the war-time poetry, insisting 'You shall not have my voice, big Voice' (*Épreuves, exorcismes*, p.13), is forced to re-emerge. The difference is that, instead of a 'Grande Voix', this is now an insidious, unobtrusive one: a language beneath language, a voiceless conspiracy to enlist and reduce. It is not a single, overpowering paternalistic God, but a merger of petty gods having taken over the psychological seats of government to regiment and condition thought: a 'take-over bid' with echoes of Prévert's authoritarian classroom scenes and their 'heads down for dictation-time' (See for example, 'Le cancre', 'Page d'écriture' or 'L'accent grave' in *Paroles*, 1949). Or it may be a more nightmarish vision of the invader, like Baudelaire's 'atrocious despot Anguish, planting its black flag in the skull' ('Spleen' in *Les Fleurs du Mal*): another totalitarian force, a malignant prophet, closing doors as it reveals the future, converting possibility into determinism; the triumph of abstraction (such as that which both threatened and galvanised the world of Camus, author of *The Plague*), thriving, like modern fascist states, on imprisonments, disappearances and oblivion. Or it may be the absolutism of time, working to impose its own defeatism: time which appears perversely to go backwards, to undo, to be synonymous with degradation and debasement; or time as the expanding shadow of Death, as it builds the inescapable prison, a *fin de siècle* to end all cycles, when time will come home to roost and the whole sequence of presents will be obliterated in the final cataclysmic one.

Almost crushed in the jaws of such threats, Michaux, again like Prévert, sketches the tenuous presence of the 'little man'. Seen as a mere puddle, a lowly blob or leftover after the great destruction, he is described nevertheless as 'infinite chance in the finiteness of cities': a meagre foreign body, a small trace of the unpredictable, within a world buttoned up. In the face of annihilation and inevitability, he becomes the grain of a tentative statement of faith: a chink of possibility, the chance element not mopped up, the possible breeding-ground for some marginal life to survive against the great uniformisation. There is, similarly, the 'limbless' nonentity, with

no 'properties' or claim on life, who, in destitution and insignificance, finds new resources, fluxes of possibility pulsing in all directions. This is another example of the mysteries of 'disconnection' and 'reconnection', of the diminution and enlargement of the self, and of the obstinate underground life of the instinct for space which, frustrated in one direction, compensates magnificently (or grotesquely, according to interpretation) in another, to make of this figure a gigantic hub, crossroads or windmill: a flail of resistance and unexpected self-affirmation.

Michaux's work is populated by 'in-between' life forms, studied as if we were witnessing the behaviour patterns of a foreign race, barely recognisable as our own. There are his 'Meidosems' (*La vie dans les plis*, pp.123-206), whose inconclusive fate is sealed in the anagrammatic 'demi-semi' of their name. The ill-defined entities of the final piece of *Dictées* also inhabit the 'space between': between *saisie* and *dessaisie*, energy and inertia. Contradictory creatures of air and earth, threatened by the bestial occupier (perhaps more frightening than the occupation forces of *Trials and exorcisms*), they aspire to higher vision and renounce higher vision. Space is their potential saviour and their tormentor, at one moment in excess, at another in dearth. And the anxious navigator of 'Sur étrave'/'At the prow' travels a restless medium between solidarity and solitude, connections and disconnections, proximity and unbridgeable distance, common quests and crossed paths, in a world of changeable signs: the perfect finale to a section entitled *Where to lay the head?*

Michaux's text has a double life. The title *Dictées* points in two directions: towards those external dictatorships which threaten and enslave the literary utterance; and towards those obscure dictations of the latent self, akin to the 'automatic writing' of the Surrealists, which are a form of liberty and a defiance of the totalitarian. These pieces show, as in the work of Rimbaud (and particularly in poems such as 'Qu'est-ce pour nous, mon cœur...' or 'Angoisse'), how poetry is forged in the battle of personal strength and weakness, and fights for its identity in the twin tensions of what Michaux calls 'the law of subordination-domination' (*Face aux verrous*, p.185).

The psychology of lines:
Children's scrawlings, children's drawings

The discovery of painting for Michaux, as a new expressive outlet, was a revelation. It was a series of new routes into himself, a switch of lines, the release of unsuspected motive forces and tempos of awareness. Above all, it was a radical disconnection from the mental processes which deal with words: a fluid, non-verbal language, not bound to the fast-congealing articulations of written expression. Michaux's writings on his own relations with the medium, 'En pensant au phénomène de la peinture'/'Thinking into the phenomenon of painting' (1946) (in *Passages*, pp.87-113) or the extensive *Émergences, résurgences/Emerge, upsurge* (1972), amply convey the ever-surprising vitality found there, the innumerable escape-routes opened for so many impulses, the sheer mobility of the shuttle-service provided, the excitement of the 'accidents' that overtake him and force him to err from his own intentions. Painting is embraced as the opposite of fixation: an astonishing phoenix born and reborn, thriving on his 'young knowledge', as it were, and on his unpreparedness. It is, he says, his 'black box' (*Émergences, résurgences*, p.45): the enigmatic flight-recorder of a journey which has 'absented' him from himself and, in its obscure discharges, provided a dynamic therapy.

Michaux's essays on other painters, from *Aventures de lignes / Linear adventures* (1954) on Paul Klee to *En rêvant à partir de peintures énigmatiques/Dreams from the enigma of painting* (1972) on René Magritte, show the two-way energy of his explorations: from the psyche into painting and from painting back into the psyche, from self to other and from other back to self, from the catalytic immersion of words in paint to that of paint in words. It is interesting, in view of the present study *Essais d'enfants, Dessins d'enfants / Children's scrawlings, children's drawings* (which David and Helen Constantine translate as *Children's ventures, Children's drawings*) to see what Michaux says (*Passages*, pp.173-80) of Klee's lines: lines going walkabout for the first time in Western painting, *trajets* rather than *objets*, trajectories rather than objects, seeking rather than finding their orientation; lines of the sub-life, penetrating rather than possessing; lines dreaming, always evading the centre while unveiling new ones.

That the universe of children's drawings should captivate the author of *Idéogrammes en Chine/Ideograms in China* (1975) and *Les ravagés/The ravaged ones* (1976), a deep disturbing communion with the paintings of the mentally ill, is not surprising. They reflect

equally his concern with the language of signs, the apparent scribblings of the misunderstood, the deciphering of 'indirections' close to origins and a first reading of the world, and the secret correlations of signs and psychology. The child's mind itself is on the verge of experience, in a stage of trial and error, still finding its tools and expressive means. Its language moves in an intermediary space, negotiating tentatively between the malleable self and an as yet unassimilated *ailleurs* or elsewhere.

Scrawled circles are its first agents: not mere doodles, but psychological lassos, looped and relooped, rehearsing a hold on the world. An infinitely open possession: forms flexibly renewed between fullness and emptiness, 'centralisation et vaporisation' (Baudelaire's phrase), 'centre et absence'. Their rhythm is repetition, as if they were caught in a self-renewing continuum, signals of a universe to be learned and relearned, in intoxicating primordial patterns, as they perform life-cycles insatiably reborn. All that revolves – tops, hoops, balls, carrousels rhythmically rising and falling – works an irresistible fascination on the child, as it does on Michaux's poetry, as seen in his images of boomerang or lasso and in the wheeling cyclic motions of a text such as 'Dans le cercle brisant de la jeune magicienne'/'In the dissolving circle of the young magician' (*Face aux verrous*, pp.241-42). The psychological importance of the circular is never more potent than in early childhood. The circle is a whole cycle of travel: departure and return, adventure and security, risk and reassurance. It is totally capacious, a vast arena for conjecture, while also a manageable container, a rounded parcel of the universe. A line is not just a line, but an inexhaustible psychic emissary. It is also an abstraction, a first tentative 'figure' launched, like poetry, to mediate between the insatiable self and a problematical reality. And its value is primarily 'gestual', invested in the act rather than the form: exploratory energy, dynamically translated, which is its own justification.

Michaux's own account is also dynamic, charting transitions, registering connections and disconnections. There comes a time when the curved line, instead of closing simply on itself, is pulled towards correspondences, gives an inkling of resemblance. And so to the emerging significance of rudimentary heads and faces (such as those which have recurrently materialised in Michaux's paintings as dark equations of the contact between the unformulated psyche and a potentially inimical 'otherness'). Heads which are often drawn out of all proportion, reflecting its prestige as the hub of so many different functions and 'agencies'. For this is not yet the begin-

ning of some slavish mimetism for the child. He is not locked on a model, nor seeking to copy. On the contrary, he is still the un-tutored 'embryologist' (as is the octogenarian Michaux, by a *mise en abyme*, or matching textual reflection, within this account): sound-ing the formative flux, its pre-natal shapes, its evolving articulations of parts and functions. He is still finding futures, ignorant of the urge for stylistic correction or 'touching up'. The comparative form-lessness of such 'portraits', with organs missing, unco-ordinated or misplaced, strikes a deep chord in Michaux's own written and pic-torial work (as well as that of a painter like Dubuffet): his bodies without body, hybrids of the visible and invisible, such as those which roam the *pays de la magie*; his filiform creatures; his *Thin man* (in *Moments/Moments*, 1973, pp.7-12). Beings summoned from the creative placenta, except that they are, as he says of the figures of Chinese theatre, 'pas *en chair*, mais à l'état *de tracé*' (*Un barbare en Asie*, p.185): that is, traced in outline, non-naturalistic, dispensed from the need to depict the whole, unhitched from the irrelevance of matter. What is then captured, in these sausage shapes and clown-ish forms, balloon-men and stick-insects, is not a particular man or a correspondent of reality, but an intuition of the essence of man: something akin to what Michaux calls *le fantomisme* (*Passages*, pp. 92-93), the painting of an inner double rather than the actual nose and eyes, 'man according to his inner dynamics' as he says in *Emerge, upsurge* (p.50). That such sketches should appear unresembling and ludicrous to the adult eye is of no consequence. All that counts is the act of transmission: the line as *fil conducteur* conveying, not the outside world as such, but the energetic movements of a formative inner world making contact with it and feeling out its correspon-dences. This, compared with the period of mere circles, is a cru-cial step, never to be retraced, towards 'representational' art. But it is still an intermediate stage – hence its attraction for Michaux – between the fluid and the fixed. It is still 'saved', so to speak, by the fact that hierarchies are not yet sealed, and men and trees, for instance, can belong to the same order; by the spontaneous power of *rapprochement* (the imaginative area of the *comme* explored by a poet such as Michel Deguy as seen, for instance, in 'Le journal du poème' in *Gisants*, 1985); by a susceptibility to magic, by which the line can act directly on the world, like the mantras or magic formulae of Indian spiritual traditions; by the uninhibited appetite for play, a 'ludic' exaltation enhanced by the child's lack of adroit-ness, which favours a humour of omission, disproportion and re-contextualisation; and above all by an extraordinarily creative *dis-*

ponibilité or 'availability' which allows the nascent artist to play, so negligently, with notions of closeness and distance, recognition and foreignness, in this half-way house between *engagement* and *dégagement*, commitment and non-commitment.

Next, in this dual 'history of art', comes the discovery of colours. What Michaux says of his own first awareness of watercolours (*Passages*, pp.108-110) is illuminating: the sudden 'flash photography', the colours moving like fish on a sheet of water or thrown as bait to bring things to the surface, the little heap decomposing into travelling particles, the deviations and the dam-busting, the innumerable passages rather than the final halt, the art of the 'moving image' like cinema, the unimpeded outlet of emotional impetus, splashed about, as in action-painting, in the blood-letting of his roaming reds. For the child, colour is the door opening on an unknown feast, beckoning beyond the schematic outlines of black and white. It is a life-force, in all its pristine vigour (welling, one might say, from the sources of Baudelaire's *Correspondances* or Rimbaud's *Voyelles*): the immediate translator of intensity of sensation and impact of perception, a responsive keyboard for a host of ambitious psychological urges in their pre-solid states. An obsessive colour can become a private vehicle, almost a magic carpet, carrying the child, as privileged traveller, through a ductile universe where all is wide-eyed discovery. The child's faith in the miraculous thrives on this pictorial megalomania, which sees everything writ large, extravagant, transfigured. What need for the visionary surprises of mescalin? It is not that the child's mind is all innocence. Indeed, there are obscurities, ambiguities and suspect undercurrents feeling their way to expression: a shifting hidden continent. But there is a disarming *bonhomie* in these shapes and faces: something humorously clownish (like the character Plume) with no malicious intent, hostility or threat, as if the child can, at this stage of his evolution, defuse the world by a natural grace, as opposed to Michaux's arduous and tormented poetic 'interventions'. Compared with the brooding and lacerated primitivism of those of the author's own painting, these open, 'available' faces represent a sort of paradise lost. Perhaps it is because the child is a natural believer, a credulous playmate of the irrational, the fanciful and the surreal. He is avid for improbables, in love with myths and narrative tales which are adventures: unlimited movement towards, the unfurling of 'elsewheres'. His coloured paintings, which already tell stories before he can speak intelligibly, are the domain of the *merveilleux* (in the sense intended by André Breton), where the possible and the impossible,

29

the real and the unreal, 'cease to be perceived contradictorily' as Breton writes in the first Surrealist Manifesto of 1924, and form, on the contrary, a natural and necessary psychological partnership. The child inhabits a miraculous composite space, recording with the utmost immediacy and ubiquity its unlikely pairings: the matter-of-fact with the extraordinary, the seen with the unseen, the physical with the mental, the object with the concept, all apprehended simultaneously. The child's mind is the supreme space-maker. It always has space in reserve, room to spare. Again one returns to the notion of the potency of lack. It is because of the child's 'missing parts', underdeveloped senses and deficiencies that it projects and re-projects itself into a thousand 'othernesses', embracing and espousing each in turn – until such time as the mould will harden, and the need for space will vanish, together with that magical sixth sense, the 'sens du manque'.

It is significant that Michaux does not choose to end his study by taking this pictorial evolution into adulthood. In this sense, it ends on a threshold. More importantly his last note is not that of infinite access, superabundance and self-enlargement. On the contrary, he turns to those less open children who, on the verge of life, flinch from its enigmas and threatening overtures. And, for these, painting is not so much an exploratory possession of the world as a defence against it, a resistance movement, a tensile retreat. Instead of the agent of an accelerating identification with the outside, it becomes a private weapon for arresting that impetus and guarding rather than compromising one's inner space. So, Michaux's study is caught to the last between alternative movements: acceptance and refusal, openness and closure. This non-participation he sees as being far more common than is generally realised: an autistic withdrawal and self-containment stemming from the difficulties of making the transition from *non-événement* to *événement*, from non-event to event, from that rounded, sufficient oneness with the maternal source to the need to acquire skills, to disperse and fragment. Such clenched states are not rare in Michaux's world: it is said, for instance, in the semi-autobiographical 'Portrait of A.', that 'right up to the brink of adolescence he formed an adequate, hermetically sealed ball, a dense, obscure and personal world where nothing entered.' (*Plume*, p.108). But they are no less rich for all that. Indeed, this realm of silent refusal, of apparent 'retarded development', is perhaps a more productive zone for exploration: seething with resources, alive with compensatory movements, solving complex equations, responding to different rhythms and tempos – all of which

make the paintings of such subjects an even more compelling visual language, whose messages lurk taciturnly at several removes.

It is a nice artistic touch that this extensive journey into children's painting, which is, for the eighty year old Michaux, a vastly empathetic journey back upstream, a return to origins, should end with the emphasis on those who, within that sphere, have declined the invitation to an unwelcome change of life and have delved back inwards to find their sustenance.

Taken by storm

To be taken by surprise, to test himself in the disruptive, is not new to Michaux's work. *Par surprise/ By surprise* is a text begun in midstream, already under pressure, conveying urgency, disquiet and pulses of 'foreignness' on the mind and syntax alike. The impact is all the more alienating in that the substance swallowed has been taken with no reason in mind, almost distractedly, so exaggerating the sense of the accidental and gratuitous. There is already an *écart*: a mind somewhere else, caught unawares by this tyrannical change of direction. Again the idea of *La nuit remue*, stirrings in the dark, comes into play: even if the 'dark' here is simply the blank of consciousness, the lapse of attention, which lets in the potency of this packet of powder found, like Baudelaire's overwhelming perfume-bottle (see 'Le flacon' in *Les Fleurs du Mal*), in the bottom of an old drawer.

Michaux's poetry is confrontational, as his title *Affrontements* (1986) testifies. Antagonistic claims meet head on, destined to thrash out equations. It is from such clashes, 'engagements' in an almost martial sense, that his writings derive so much of their energy, nervous instability and resourcefulness. He is abnormally alert to the encroachments of invisible enemies (such as the 'jelly-fish of the air' or the destructive sound-waves in the silent 'echo-arena' in the Magic Land): enemies which defy all hand-hold and contemptuously jostle the constituted self, its traditional prerogatives, its defensive properties. The forces of 'depersonalisation' are always at the gate, like waves on a shore-line, eroding ownership, redefining frontiers, forcing new accommodations on the *moi* – which is not a fixture, a reliability, a circumscribed definition, but a disputed zone, constantly at risk, porous, subject to exchange and interchange, alternately probing and retreating, asserting and negating, not only in its precarious position between *dedans* and *dehors*, within and without, but, more problematically, between conflicting orientations of the *dedans*.

As the mind is dislodged from its positions, so is the style and expression: with sudden fluctuations and spasms of intensification, incomplete sentences which do not quite acquire coherence, fitful transitions, cellular disturbances. The text as journey: of somewhat soluble composition, with mini-leaps and transfers, prone to 'elsewheres' which spring their own surprises and displacements on the reading experience.

All the hallmarks of Michaux's poetry are here: a reality which leaps out of its falsely congealed postures, restored, as in a Bergsonian vision, to its authentic mobility; *élan vital*, pure impetus travelling, not to go anywhere or vanish into its destination, but simply to replenish itself and perpetuate departure; vision rendered infinitely acute and infinitely extensive, the more so because of his role as 'foreigner', alive with signs where once was sullen surface and not yet absorbed into patterns of significance. Above all, there is a crisis of space, as if his so-called 'real' space, a mere mental box now threatened with explosion, were not made to house such intensity. Time, too, is massively enlarged, beyond his petty tempos, beyond any controllable *frame* of mind. It is also a lurch beyond images, visual or mental, as they are outpaced and erased by the abstraction of sheer movement.

One sees the mental world, its strongholds, its conglomerations, its schemes of self-protection, dramatically under assault. And, with them, those of language: thrown back into the melting-pot, destructured, literally disconcerted and frantically seeking to regroup and re-form. It is in pieces such as *By surprise* that one realises the extent to which a study of drugs is also, for Michaux, a study of the engine-room of poetry. Rimbaud's 'reasoned derangement of all the senses' springs to mind (see his letter to Paul Demeny, 15 May 1871, known as the 'lettre du voyant'). For certainly there is 'dérèglement', of the most radical kind, and certainly it is 'raisonné', in the form of analysis seeking to steer a course, alternately (if not simultaneously) submerged and resurfacing, knowing attacks and remissions. It is indeed the essence of Michaux's genius to be the fine-shaded analyst, tracking his inner movements with microscopic accuracy, while conveying 'live' the turbulences of an experience which undermines all analysis and makes it impossible. Michaux said (in R. Bréchon, *Michaux*, Gallimard, 1959, p.21) that his early journeys were essentially 'voyages d'expatriation', deliberately undertaken to break links with the over-constricting familiarity of one culture. The present 'displacement' is more a forcible expulsion, but its effects are the same: the anguish of missing communications,

as if one were forever clutching at vanishing life-lines, even though thrown by oneself; the restlessness of changing directions, with one stimulus and attempted response already countered and superseded by another; the uncompromising exposure of the multi-vocal self, tormented by irreconcilable voices; the sense of ineptitude, as the sum of one's 'apprenticeships' in life and one's accumulated resources are left stranded; the realisation that loss of balance is not a single state, but the disruption of innumerable balances, all interconnected like those of a watch.

The text is once more a 'space between', alive with contradictory impulses: a fast breeder of opposites, dangerously overheating. The centripetal and the centrifugal, will and disintegration of the will, starkly imprinted details and erasures, dictatorial affirmations and instant negations, the most violent physical hammer-blows and mental vacuities, write and rewrite the tenuous equation which was Michaux. The more one tries to form a circuit of thought, the more it is broken and frustrated. The end in mind is dissolved in the approach. One cannot settle for one option or the other. The 'self' is nothing but one precarious resultant after another. Even the *event* of which he is the undeniable victim, after so many reversals and eclipses, can no longer be ascertained as having taken place. The assumed cause of his present state – the forgotten drug in the drawer – may just as easily be its *effect*, the mere projection or invention of his feverish condition. The demarcation-lines between reality and fiction, the *vraisemblable* and the *invraisemblable* (these being the frontiers of all writing and every literary act), can no longer be taken for granted. Strangely, the 'evidence' of particular detail becomes the very proof of its falseness – a wishful crystallisation of the mind, clutched as a life-raft – while absence of reality is the truth. Even a wall, the epitome of solids, while indubitably there before the eye, is essentialised beyond matter, 'abstracted' from itself. The actual becomes virtual, and vice versa, incessantly. Concrete and abstract, physical and metaphysical, radically challenge each other's definition and raison d'être.

Other opposites, affecting the viability and ultimately the justification of the literary act, emerge from the confrontation. For, though taken by storm and in so many ways annulled, the experimentalist is lucid, flexible and resistant in proportion to the ingenuities of the onslaught. Each negative forces its positive to the surface. 'At least let's take advantage of the state,' he declares. In the first instance, this means the amazed discovery of the immeasurable system of checks and balances, mechanisms of adjustment, articu-

lations of moving parts and dependencies, pressure-points and re-distribution routes, which is the human mind; and how many different wavelengths and frequencies one can manipulate when thrown open to an influx of new signals. 'What a fantastic machine is man' (*Connaissance par les gouffres/Knowledge via the abyss*, 1961, p.155), he says in one of his major accounts of the 'laboratory' of mescalin. Clearly, Michaux's work does not represent the romanticism of drugs. 'Drugs and their paradise are a bore,' he maintains, 'Let them give us instead a bit of knowledge. Ours is not a century of paradises.' (*Connaissance par les gouffres*, p.9). There is no idle transcendentalism or ecstatic abandonment. The emphasis is on his inner workshop, its versatile equipment, the sharpness of its analytical tools, its high degree of output. And his experience of the metaphysical, undergone to the extreme, replaces the dreaming and other-worldliness of nineteenth-century poetry with clash and the wiles of conquest. One sees the multiplication of the self and its extraordinary powers of self-observation: a kind of meta-lucidity, in which he is his own spectacle, with one function of the brain watching the brain at work. ('Je est un autre,' Rimbaud has said in his 'lettre du voyant' or 'letter of the seer'.). One sees also the other side of the victim's 'unreadiness': the fascination, when one has been caught unawares and the mind is in disarray, of summoning up unrealised, unprecedented resources. Writing is never exhausted, for Michaux, as a counter-measure. It forms pockets of resistance, seeks out points of leverage and defensive reinforcements. It breeds vigilance, unexpected flexibilities and speeds of intervention. It is a freedom-fighter: freedom seen not as a state, but as a never-ending series of actions won against threat and negation.

At the same time, the language machine is forced to new flexibilities and proofs of its stamina. The incomplete sentences and arrests; the suddenly bristling questions; the parentheses and voices from the wings; the complex articulations of clauses and sub-clauses, centres and margins; the gear-changes and modifications of tempo; the variable densities and fluctuating emphases: all reflect, with dynamic immediacy, the efforts of language to come to terms with the alternating currents of what is at the same time its destroyer and its stimulus. Language here is a frontier-exercise: between the more and the less conscious, coherence and incoherence, degrees of detachment and savage involvement. These new formations and crystallisations, somehow maintaining their mobility and creative freshness, rise up improbably from the paradoxical excitement of relinquishing one's authority while battling to safeguard it, of

watching one's frameworks dismantled while frantically fashioning emergency ones.

A postscript, *Lendemains / Mornings after* follows the main text, giving it a bi-partite structure. Written after the event, when the world has fallen back into habitable categories, with dividing lines firmly in place and surfaces holding good, it prolongs the experience's 'double-life' in time. Whereas, in the original text, he was racked by the discrepancy between the measurements of wrist-watch time and the awesomely enlarged time of the drug perception which could not be pulled together, now, in this seemingly peripheral footnote, an even greater discrepancy looms large, harder still to reconcile: that between the six months of difficult, intermittent labour taken to write this account, and a densely continuous experience, defiant of words, which took place at staggering speed in only a few hours. The key would seem to be that Michaux had kept the event secret, taking no notes, speaking of it to no one. In this way, undivulged, never congealed into verbal equivalents which would adulterate and imprison it, it has retained the vigour of its underground life, an evolving virtuality for expression. So, again like Baudelaire's perfume-bottle (see 'Le flacon', second stanza), its latent creativity has been amplified by a period of neglect. More significantly, the image of the forgotten packet of drug retrieved from an old drawer is superseded by its more essential parallel: namely, the experience itself surging back from half-oblivion, to prove that it has not yet expended itself as *terra incognita* but has a new extended life to exercise. The secretive operations of memory have not been short-circuited. In this way, the experience resurrects itself in a new light, according to a maturing definition in time. It has not lost the power to become its own opposite. What once seemed like a dispossession, a rape, a spoliation, is now revalued as a generosity unjustifiably granted, an inestimable gift. And now, in its absence, it is perhaps more densely and influentially present. It has, it seems, unlimited aftermaths, richer and more miraculous than its violent actuality. And the text ends, at a point where it is again part of a world sealed into tight compartments, on unfurling conjecture and ever-changing vision.

It has not been readily appreciated to what extent Michaux's work, like that of Proust, sets itself *à la recherche du temps perdu*. *By surprise* represents just such a quest, in several distinct ways. Lost time, in the sense of being disconnected from the safety of chronological markers and of needing to fight one's way back, is central to the piece. At another level, it is via the literary act that

the author is pursuing time lost, attempting to repossess it up to six months after the event. Beyond that, however, he has the sense of having, in the process, gone back to origins, to the very sources of time, not only through his own ages but those of all human evolution, to be rejoined with a primeval time or temporal infinity.

One should emphasise, finally, the supreme paradox of the enterprise: that, in spite of a *décalage* or discrepancy of times by which the literary act is irreparably, irretrievably, behind the train of the experience in question, Michaux's text re-opens its 'present' with an immediacy of perception, vitality of movement and flexibility of tempo which completely mask any temporal difference. Just as, in the throes of the crisis, real time and mental time were eventually brought back into harness, so, in the literary experience, two seemingly incompatible times are made to coincide with an extraordinary vibrancy. By what mysterious *passages*, one might ask, has the writer found his way back with such remarkable powers of identification? How has he bridged the abyss between experience and its narration? What *literary* drug or fluid, more efficacious than the original, has reconnected him, turning the inevitable *dégagement* into a miracle of restored contact?

Into Infinity

Where *By surprise* is the arena of violence and energies at loggerheads, *Le jardin exalté/ The heavenly garden* is, by some unexplained turn of the circle, the journey to euphoria and universal harmony. The transition illustrates again the rapid changeability of Michaux's exploratory world, its restless alternations and counterweights, its varied avenues of mental projection. After the 'turbulent infinity' (see also the text entitled *L'infini turbulent*, 1957), the ecstatic infinity.

The heavenly garden starts in a flat, unemotional tone: an apparent detachment with regard to the taking of the drug which will better accentuate the exaltation which will shortly send the experience soaring. It also starts, as does *Journey that keeps at a distance*, with a criss-cross of perspectives: he who approached the experiment with equanimity suffering an adverse reaction, while a woman companion, who was initially apprehensive, finds herself unusually relaxed. Not only does this set against each other greater or lesser degrees of expansion and contraction, acceptance and refusal, but it shows how the same experience can veer in different directions, sometimes the most unlikely ones, according to different subjectivities

and moods and circumstances of the moment. It also allows Michaux, in the first instance, to be someone else's observer, watching the onset of symptoms on *her* face, juxtaposing his consciousness with her unselfconsciousness, in another two-sided experience with its *endroit* and *envers*, its recto and verso, its actor and spectator.

What he witnesses are the signs of an extended communication: both with regard to external reality, in that the woman's visual perceptions are newly alert and alive, and with each other, in that they seem spontaneously to read each other's thoughts and share a confidence with no reserves. What surges to life above all is her face, opened up, activated as never before: an expressive universe, passing at speed through a gamut of tendencies and orientations, psychological times and temptations, flexible beyond belief. The simplicity of a single self, fixed in the habitual features and arbitrarily maintained, disintegrates; and a host of alternative, complementary, competing selves emerge from their under-nourishment in this new liberal regime and jostle for precedence. One better understands, in this context, the shifting faces of Michaux's own painting. They are the hidden selves of a life-time, psychological possibilities devalued at the expense of others, abandoned at a crossroads, starved by stronger appetites, victims of some more compelling choice. But they have never been jettisoned, nor effectively exorcised. They are part of that *vie dans les plis*, the lurking life of the underside, which patiently awaits its opportunities. In the woman's mobile features, it is as if all those residual and potential selves were being realised, not one by one, but simultaneously, in one fell swoop. A release all the more liberal in that neither she nor he can think to apply it, draw advantage from it, harness or analyse it: a *play* of masks, in the sense of play as expression for its own sake, with no goal in mind and no conceivable use.

At this juncture, the writer is still an outsider, living this vast mobilisation by proxy, as it were, while himself undergoing continued physical malaise. It is nevertheless a threshold already crossed: an empathetic 'translation' elsewhere, a visible prelude to his own immersion. All this needs is an adjustment of position, an increased physical relaxation, and the right music (in this case oriental) to induce self-abandonment and receptivity. Again the potency of music is celebrated: music as supreme solvent, penetrating resistance, breaking barriers; music with a fluid intimacy, entering and espousing the 'space within'; music indefinitely expansive, always having come from somewhere and bound for somewhere else, transporting the self like a tiny grain; music as the magic mediator (as per-

fume was for Baudelaire) between outer and inner worlds, sense and spirit, existence and essence; music which has shed matter and left the referential world, bearing the quintessence of the 'inner force' of India and fusing it with his own; music as liquid movement, permeating inwards while spilling further and further afield towards greater grandeur; music enveloping all with its oneness, transcending persons and places, abolishing conflicts and discrepancies, dissolving one's petty, private horizons into the universal.

A blank in the text, one line of dots, marks another threshold. It is a totally porous 'passage', from which all explanation, analysis or verbal apprehension is missing. It offers no resistance. It is atemporal, of unspecified duration: it can be infinitely extensive or felt as virtually instantaneous, time long or time short. Beyond it, he and the music are an indistinguishable sea.

External reality is not obliterated, however, by this inner transport. On the contrary, the music works inwards and remoulds the perceptive consciousness, only to work outwards again: union without limit, embracing perfectly inner and outer worlds. And, before one's very eyes, an ordinary country garden, with no special grace or merit, is miraculously transmuted, with, as its centrepiece, its 'crowning glory', a huge tree in movement: its twin crown not simply symbolising, but actually realising, the reconciliation of dualities. Firmly rooted in the ground but a dance of animated foliage, it is *entre centre et absence* (see *Plume*, pp.36-37), solidity and dissolution, sameness and infinite invention. It is the inexhaustible mediator of earth and air, surface and depth, visible and invisible, horizontal and vertical, perennity and rebirth, the eternal and the transient, self-enclosure and dissemination, weight and weightlessness. It is also, in this case, the perfect union of art and nature, permeated as it is by this all-pervasive music fusing mind and matter.

The garden itself becomes the ultimate garden, a paradise on earth, where all quests end. But there is no stasis. Incessant motion animates and re-animates, opening threshold beyond threshold, reawakening desire beyond desire. Sensual and abstract, physical and metaphysical, here and elsewhere, self and other find total partnership. The absolute overflows itself in constant replenishment. Paul Valéry's distinction between prose as *la marche* and poetry as *la danse*, between walking and dancing, comes to fruition: pure expressivity of movement, supreme pliability and grace infusing the world, delighting in itself for itself. In the gentle but imperative rhythmic alternations, possession and dispossession, arrival and departure, gift and withdrawal, fulfilment and renewed desire are made one.

Things part only to re-embrace, bow down only to soar back upwards, fade only to re-emerge. Each part becomes a whole, and the whole is translated into every part. No particle is inert or passive: each is a life-force, each a universe. Leaves and branches of the extremity are the levitational translation of the centre, reminding one of Pascal's ultimate sphere 'whose circumference is nowhere and centre everywhere' (*Pensées*, Lafuma edition, p.199).

There is no doubt that this piece is one of the most prolonged climaxes in Michaux's writing. His expression is drawn back and back to the subject, with a repetitive fullness, enthusiasm, phonetic richness and verbal delight rare in the work of this often spare, clenched and resistant author. A superlative lyricism is sustained, expanded and expanding, as if it, too, were a proliferation of active parts, individually animated and impassioned, but borne in an all-embracing tide surging to one end. It is hard to imagine paragraphs more intimately moulded, more excited, more uplifted by the fluctuations of rhythm than these: upward and downward, to and fro, furling and unfurling motions joining as one, simultaneously desirous and ecstatic, sensuous and sacred, energetic and serene. Wave after wave, pulse after pulse, the text is quenched and unquenched, made instantly available to a further beyond: 'inlassable dépassement', endlessly superseding itself. And significantly, this supreme felicity takes place 'between Earth and Heavens': not belonging to one or the other, but created and recreated in the space between, where no boundary applies or can even be conceived, a space of universal invitation which is the guarantee of infinite transgression and boundless correspondence.

Michaux adds a slightly curious touch to 'finish': curious in that it *is* added, as if an extraneous extra or small supplement to the perfection evoked, and not quite intrinsic to it. It is the mention of the emergence of a rhythmic beat, as if coming from the innermost heart of the tree. But nothing is on the wane. This becomes yet another 'contradiction' to join, enrich and excel all other opposites so consummately fused: the seemingly peripheral which is the very *heart* of the matter, the additional which is the essential, the barely perceptible which is the all-encompassing. For this is the very heartbeat of the tree, its life-source, its centre; and not just of the tree, however enlarged and transfigured, but, through it, of the whole of the vegetal world and the planet itself, the secret scansion of the universe. The cliché of 'two hearts beating as one' is realised superlatively: the emotion of the world and the emotion of the self, the music of the man and the music of nature, outer and inner, the

private and the cosmic, joined in an unsurpassable (yet constantly self-surpassing) harmony.

What has been temporarily exorcised here, supremely, miraculously, is the Michaux of inner torments and frustrated quests: the man of daggers and broken bottle-ends, of holes and ghosts: the eternal traveller who writes from the hinterland and places of exile, saying, 'And still they held me back, keeping me from my homeland' (*Face aux verrous*, p.236) or 'The boat would not leave, with me on board could never leave' (*Face aux verrous*, p.240); or the rebel and alien who, in *Qu'il repose en révolte/ May he rest in revolt*, composes this epitaph for himself: 'In the twisted arms of desires forever unfulfilled shall he be remembered' (*La vie dans les plis*, p.118). Hardly so.

Positions of the self

After the exaltation of *The heavenly garden*, the collection comes to an end in more modest perspectives and more piecemeal, provisional achievements. And after two passages inspired by drugs, one which goes wrong and the other which goes right, but both of which record an invasion and dissolution of the will, the final group of texts returns to a more volitional, self-orientated mood, so reinforcing what Michaux says in the postface to *Plume* (1938): 'I would like to have been a good head of laboratory, and be thought to have managed my "self" effectively' (p.212).

The title *Postures*, while perhaps emphasising an element of artifice and contrivance, or at least poses artificially sustained, reinforces a more important theme: the countless changing positions adopted by the self. As he writes in the same postface: 'There is not one self. There are not ten selves. Self does not exist. SELF is merely a point of equilibrium' (*Plume*, p.213). All of Michaux's work is concerned with delicate points of balance, and all that can hinge on them. The occult practices of his Magic Land are directed towards tapping and controlling the volatile field of force which is their domain: exercises of mind over matter, psychic interventions, the projection outwards of inner stresses as visible 'figures' in the outside world – all performed as a means of regulating the unbalanced, relieving incompatibilities, compensating for deficiencies, bolstering the waning or hesitant (or simply the 'natural') resources of personality. The 'Magi' themselves are a fictional projection of examples of exceptional self-control gleaned from Michaux's jour-

ney through Asia. For, in *A barbarian out East,* he speaks of Indians who 'give the sense of intervening somewhere within, in a way that you are incapable of' (p.17); describes the Hindu as a person 'reinforced by meditation, a being to the power of two' (p.37), and is struck by the prevalent belief in psychic energies and the efficacy of magic. He comments on a chart illustrating the different '*attitudes* of prayer', alongside a statue of Kali; and lists as one of the most astonishing sights of the whole itinerary, the inflated belly of his *guru yogi,* controlling and channelling respiration, converting it into currents of spiritual strength and well-being: a man who was 'above human misery, inaccessible rather than indifferent, of almost invisible goodness' (p.82). Few writers have travelled as extensively the geography of the body as Michaux: its trigger-spots, its secret networks of communication, its mysterious complicities with movements of the mind. And few have been led to delve so searchingly, in this case through illness, into the interactions, beneficial or detrimental, between bodily positions and states of mind in need of alleviation and relief.

The first 'posture' described is essentially a circular one. Physically, it starts simply from arms and hands, with fingers crossed, joined behind the head, surrounding and cradling it: a circle around a circle, like a halo or, perhaps more appropriately, a widening reverberation ready to release further concentric circles. This 'natural magic of a mere pose', as he calls it, seals him from the world at large, creating another 'buffer-zone', as it were, different from those of the imaginative countries of *Ailleurs/Elsewhere* (1948). It is serenely self-embracing. It makes a 'disconnection' from the antagonisms, importunities, irritants and disruptions of an agitated and futile external reality. It switches from one circuit, with its cacophony of false messages, doctrinaire pronouncements, slogans and simplistic linguistic commerce, to another, where all such imperatives are muffled and remote, and one is acquitted from the need for prudence, calculation, strategic thinking, the weighing of pros and cons and the deliberate mobilisation of resources. It puts one 'out of circulation', but only to restore one, motionless, to the indivisible, to continuity without end. It is an 'abstraction' of a sort, and a form of 'abstinence': one abstains from intervention, one abstains from the excesses of self, one abstains from properties and possession, one abstains from one's own peripheries. All that is trivial and redundant is shed. And, free from distractions and deviations, one rediscovers centrality. The uncertainty and frustration of the experience of the Magic Land, where the 'Federal Capital'

remains forever elusive *(Ailleurs,* p.192), or of the *espace aux ombres / space of shadows*, tormented by the question 'Surely there must be something other than accidents...there must be some *being*' *(Face aux verrous*, pp.176-77), are quelled: 'So there was really a capital somewhere inside!' he exclaims. The author of 'Je vous écris d'un pays lointain'/'I write from a distant land' and 'Nouvelles de l'étranger'/ 'News from abroad' now receives no news, no further messages, from the 'provinces', the further reaches of his outstretched body. And what, in the *pays de la magie*, was a challenge and a test of strength, namely to walk at once on both sides of a stream *(Ailleurs,* p.167), is here magnificently accomplished: a huge bridge spanning an immeasurable river, in one great sweep or parabola of the now-inhabited circle, epitomising the transcendence of opposites and infinity of communication. Fasting is a return to the essential, a self-stripping, a cleansing of the system, the creation of a void within: which becomes, in turn, a space within, a vacancy, *vacance* as holiday or holy-day, a blessed reprieve from the superfluities of the everyday and re-admittance to one's true element (or aliment).

The first position is called 'privileged posture'. It has echoes in numerous circular figures in Michaux's work, but not all of which reflect the same mood or modus operandi: the bristling curling up on himself like a defensive hedgehog; the hypnotic focus of 'an eye like Aum' *(La vie dans les plis*, p.90); the sudden frozen tranquillity of placing himself inside an apple *(Plume*, pp.9-10); or the perfect ball of his alter ego A. where, it is said, 'he sustained himself with nothing, keeping to a bare but solid minimum, and feeling the movements within of great convoys of mysterious matter' *(Plume*, p.108). And, even if some of the derived sensations may seem identical – continuity, appeasement, transfusion, purification, unity – none of these circles is the same, any more than the child's drawn loops. Each is a new universe, with its own psychological moment and necessities. The form, moreover, is different: the perfect disclaimer to those who would say, 'A circle is a circle is a circle'. For the *form* is the *mode*. And in the case of *Postures*, the circular experience engenders a unique spacious expression not found elsewhere in the collection: a flowing river, advancing in wavelets, with expansion and contractions, accelerations and decelerations, traversed by momentary metaphors formed and reformed at the fringe of the imagination only to be lost, in this rhythmic massage which is a seemingly tireless spiritual 'toning'.

But there is nothing definitive for Michaux about the circle, however 'privileged' its virtues, any more than there is in the spiral,

which some critics have seen as his dominant motif. *Posture No 2*, for instance, finds a quite different direction from the same recumbent position. Here, instead of ease, calm and fluid receptivity, the stylistic vibrations produce a state of tension and pent-up energy, and the repetitions become the pulse of a gathering momentum. This is the martial Michaux, the resistance man, highly charged, galvanised. And the circle, which previously dissolved all that was angular, is replaced by the triangle and its pointed thrust. Such sudden condensations of force are common in Michaux. In a poem entitled 'Dragon' he writes, 'A dragon came out of me. A hundred tails of flames and nerves he came' (*L'espace du dedans/The space within*, 1966, p.252). In 'Bonheur bête'/'Meek happiness' (*La nuit remue*, pp.49-50), he laments that contentment has snapped all impetus and in-vokes the return of misery, with its resistances and more dynamic objectives; while in 'Étapes'/'Stages along the way' (*La nuit remue*, pp.47-48) he concludes, on a similar theme, 'They took away my lightning. They tore out my nails and teeth. And they gave me an egg to hatch.' In numerous poems he assumes the characteristics of missile or projectile. In the 'epitaph' of 'May he rest in revolt' his memory is engraved in 'the whistling departure of the tracer bullet' (*La vie dans les plis*, p.116); in *Movements* he adopts the image of 'man bent like a bow...for operation lightning for operation harpoon' (*Face aux verrous*, p.10); while in *Trials and exorcisms*, not only does he describe the process of exorcism as 'arrow-like flight' and 'explosive upsurge', but he speaks of his body, charged by a grimly determined and recalcitrant humour, as 'shot from a cannon' (pp. 7-12). In this second 'posture', the triangle becomes just such a missile. It still implies a reduction of the world, an abstraction, an elimination of extraneous matter, as, mentally, he recoils into the apex of a triangle (in the corner of the room behind him). It still provides a vast realisation of space, but now with a new tautness, speed and propulsive power. So much that his 'capsule' becomes detached from the whole and 'pulls away', beyond all bearings and physical landmarks, and he hurtles off with incredible force as if strapped in the backward-facing seat of a space-probe. This is another dramatic illustration of Michaux's unending exploration of the hidden motors of experience, and of himself as *transformer*. Here, in this irresistible 'movement towards', there is nothing faltering or hesistant. The whole being becomes, not a thing of reverie or vague aspiration, but a living power-house: though sedentary, a burning nucleus of impetus and kinetic energy, locked on its target as if by 'automatic

pilot', homing in infallibly, with no detours or deflections, in the true direction.

Postures III and *IV*, as yet more adjustments of position (the first towards a new kind of calm and buoyancy with no physical expenditure and no call for worldly exchange or intercourse; the second towards an infinite extension of time and space which abolishes differences, divisions and disparities), serve to emphasise the innumerable routes and different directions, the endless variations on a theme, the vastness of the keyboard available to Michaux in his *problème d'être*. Each 'posture', and there is no reason to suppose that the number stops here, is, if not an 'attitude of prayer', then at least an attitude of the spiritual self, delicately sought and sustained as a retreat, a balm, a beneficent elsewhere. In 'Fin d'un domaine' /'End of an estate' the fictional 'owner' says, 'Without the work of drainage and irrigation, carefully balanced and alternating, the estate suffers' (*Face aux verrous*, p.215). *Postures* represents just such a meticulous governing of the pressures and redistribution of forces to ensure the health of the domain. They are a sample of the infinite movements of the inner self, its displacements, realignments and fluctuating responses to an unstable balance of power. Fast or slow, rounded or angular, wilful or abandoned, spacious or tense, they are all, as Michaux says in the poem 'Movements': 'Signs of the ten thousand ways of seeking equilibrium in this shifting world which mocks all adaptations...Signs, not to be complete, but to be faithful to the "transitory" within' (*Face aux verrous*, p.20). They are dynamic expressions of the poet's 'ductile universe' (the phrase of the critic Richard Ellmann): Michaux the Meidosem, elastic man, man in between, whose experience is all transits and frontiers.

'If there are people more supple than me, I'd be surprised,' he writes in *Façons d'endormi, façons d'éveillé/ Waking ways, sleeping ways* (1969, p.214). Nothing could illustrate this better than the collection *Spaced, displaced*: poetry changing its shapes, redefining its identity, finding new passages, insatiably metamorphic, as it ventures into uncharted zones of perception and understanding.

Bibliography

1. Michaux's Major Works

Qui je fus (Paris: Gallimard, 1927).

Ecuador (Paris: Gallimard, 1929).

Un barbare en Asie (Paris: Gallimard, 1933).

La nuit remue (Paris: Gallimard, 1935).

Plume, précédé de *Lointain intérieur* (Paris: Gallimard, 1938).

Épreuves, exorcismes (Paris: Gallimard, 1945).

Ailleurs (*Voyage en Grande Garabagne, Au Pays de la Magie, Ici Poddema*) (Paris: Gallimard, 1948).

La vie dans les plis (Paris: Gallimard, 1949).

Face aux verrous (Paris: Gallimard, 1954).

Misérable miracle (Monaco: Éditions du Rocher, 1956, then Paris: Gallimard, 1972).

L'infini turbulent (Paris: Mercure de France, 1957 and 1964).

Passages (Paris: Gallimard, 1950 and 1963).

Connaissance par les gouffres (Paris: Gallimard, 1961).

Les grandes épreuves de l'espirit (Paris: Gallimard, 1966).

L'espace du dedans: pages choisies 1927-59 (Paris: Gallimard, 1966).

Façons d'endormi, façons d'éveillé (Paris: Gallimard, 1969).

Émergences, résurgences (Geneva: Skira, 1972).

Face à ce qui se dérobe (Paris: Gallimard, 1974).

Choix de poèmes (Paris: Gallimard, 1976).

Poteaux d'angle (Paris: Gallimard, 1981).

Chemins cherchés, chemins perdus, transgressions (Paris: Gallimard, 1981).

Déplacements Dégagements (Paris: Gallimard, 1985).

Affrontements (Paris: Gallimard, 1986).

2. Michaux Texts in English Translation

A barbarian in Asia, translated by Sylvia Beach (New York: New Directions, 1949).

The space within, translated by Richard Ellmann (New York: New Directions, 1951).

Miserable miracle, translated by Louise Varese (San Francisco: City Lights, 1963).

Light through darkness, translated by Haakon Chevalier (New York: Orion Press, 1963).

Henri Michaux, translation of 19 texts by Teo Savory (Santa Barbara: Unicorn Press, 1967).

Selected writings of Henri Michaux, translated by Richard Ellmann (New York: New Directions, 1968).

Ecuador: a travel journal, translated by Robin Magowan (Seattle: University of Washington Press, 1970).

The major ordeal of the mind and the countless minor ones, translated by Richard Howard (New York: Harcourt Brace Jovanovich, 1974).

Peace in the breaking flood, translated by Michael Fineberg (Consigny: Embers Press, 1976).

3. Further Reading on Michaux

IN ENGLISH

Malcolm Bowie: *Henri Michaux: a study of his literary works* (Oxford University Press, 1973).

Peter Broome: *Henri Michaux* (London: Athlone Press, 1977).

(*See also* Peter Broome, Introduction and notes to edition of *Au Pays de la Magie*, London: Athlone Press, 1977).

IN FRENCH

Robert Bréchon: *Michaux* (Paris: Gallimard, 1969).

René Berthelé: *Henri Michaux* (Paris: Seghers, 1972).

Les Cahiers de l'Herne (No.8): *Henri Michaux* (1983).

Jean-Michel Maulpoix: *Michaux passager clandestin* (Seyssel: Champ Vallon, 1984).

Europe (Nos.698-99): *Henri Michaux* (1987).

Une foule sortie de l'ombre

A crowd come out of the dark

J'arrive. – Je m'étais fait conduire en voiture à un local éloigné, où l'on donnait un film étranger. – La salle est grande, je le sais, une des plus grandes construites dans le pays.

Elle me parut phénoménalement grande, surtout d'un côté (le gauche) qui semblait se prolonger à n'en pas finir, effet extraordinaire.

Le spectacle déjà bien commencé, on était en pleine action. Des gens douteux sortaient de l'ombre, conspirateurs à coup sûr. Il en venait, il en venait, émergeant d'une sorte de vaste grotte, exceptionnellement vaste, espace incertain que je n'arrivais pas à délimiter.

Ils donnaient vraiment l'impression de sortir «de la bouche du néant». On n'avait jamais vu cela. Ah, me disais-je, ils font à présent des progrès au cinéma.

Faire sortir aussi naturellement des conspirateurs de l'ombre, une ombre dense, émouvante, nourrie de mystère, voilà qui n'avait jamais été réussi jusque-là.

Je ne suivais plus l'action que sur un arrière-fond de réflexions, d'interprétations, de particulière admiration, et toujours des foules sortaient de l'obscur, d'où elles semblaient se couler dans le réel. Ces ensembles mouvants n'étaient qu'une partie d'une masse plus grande, plus enfoncée, plus inquiétante. Merveille et presque miracle rendu perceptible: l'infini (d'un côté) s'abouchant de l'autre côté avec le fini et s'y écoulant!

J'étais abasourdi, comme si je m'étais trouvé au tournant même d'une époque, qui muait devant moi, et qui, grâce à une découverte nouvelle, jusque-là tenue secrète, montrait son signe neuf, là sous mes yeux.

Cependant à la sortie de la caverne le défilé n'en finissait pas, lui aussi extraordinaire et comme je n'en avais jamais vu représenter. Si attentif que je fusse à ces hommes passant en rangs plus ou moins réguliers, je ne leur voyais, me semblait-il, qu'une jambe, celle qui se portait en avant, et ne distinguais que mal une moitié du corps vaguement cachée de la même façon indéfinissable.

Vraiment on avait affaire à des conspirateurs essentiels, typiques, tels qu'on ne peut mieux les concevoir, qui par prudence et méfiance (par une expression géniale de leur méfiance) se tenaient, même en défilant, en partie dissimulés, sortant réellement

I arrive. – I had been driven, at my own request, to a remote district where they were showing a foreign film. – I am aware how large the hall is. It is one of the largest ever built in those parts.

Phenomenally large it appeared to me, especially on one side (the left) which seemed, in an extraordinary fashion, to stretch into infinity.

The film had begun, we were already well into it. Suspicious looking people were emerging from the shadows; they were plotting something, so much was obvious. More were appearing, more and more, out of a vast cave, as it seemed, an extraordinarily vast cave, an unclear zone that I could not get the measure of.

Truly, they looked to me to be issuing "out of the void". It was an unprecedented sight. Well, I said to myself, this is something new in cinema.

Never before, never with such naturalness, had conspirators been brought forth out of the darkness, out of such a dense and troubling darkness.

And now my own reflections, my interpretations and my extreme admiration became the background against which I watched the action unfold, and crowds all the while were emerging out of the dark and seemed, as they left it, to flow into reality. And these moving entities were only a part of a larger, deeper and more dis-quieting mass. Something marvellous, something almost miraculous, was being presented to my senses: infinity from one side reaching into the finite world on the other, and passing away in it.

I was dumbfounded. It was as if I were present at the turning point of an era, as if the times were set in motion and, thanks to a new discovery kept secret till then, were showing forth their novelty before my very eyes.

Meanwhile the march of men continued from the cavern's mouth, and this too, this procession, was a thing the like of which I had never seen in any film before. Though I watched very closely their more or less regular ranks they seemed, so far as I could see, each to have only one leg, the one they stepped out with, and a half of each body too could scarcely be distinguished but was vague and hidden in the same indefinable way.

These were indeed conspirators of the purest kind, none purer than these could ever be imagined; for as they left the void and ent-ered reality they were so cautious, so mistrustful and so masterly in

du vide.

Prudence justifiée sans doute, mais marche bien singulière. Peut-être pas tellement, s'agissant d'une action après tout théâtrale, qui tendait à donner l'indication qu'il s'agissait de partisans, devant par définition échapper aux regards et à la certitude.

Au déguisement soustractif et partiellement dématérialisant, comme il convient à des conspirateurs qui entendent se dissimuler le plus longtemps possible, une autre trouvaille du cinéaste prodigieux, dont je brûlais de connaître le nom, consistait à entretenir, à la faveur d'un mécanisme technique nouveau, un je ne sais quoi de vibrant, qui était du psychique pur rendu par un procédé physique. Quoi qu'il en soit, on recevait l'impression qu'on a de la vie même, de la vie en danger.

De rapides variations d'une nature inconnue, commotions à peine perceptibles, rendaient de façon admirable l'appréhension d' hommes en danger et ces alternances d'audace et de peur que doit ressentir une troupe préparant un coup de main et une attaque par surprise, émotions qui vont au cœur et ne se discutent pas.

J'étais là bien plus que spectateur. Relié de force, je me sentais sur les lieux, avec eux. Je ne l'avais jamais été autant. Je manquais seulement du pouvoir de les toucher, et encore. Par moments, j'avais un recul, tant je sentais réel leur mouvement.

Jamais un spectacle ne m'avait comme celui-ci rendu présent, participant, engagé.

Ma vie de spectateur venait de trouver un rebondissement spectaculaire. Sans l'avoir prévu, j'étais entré dans l'époque suivante. J'admirais et soliloquais.

Soudain une pénétrante douleur m'arrête, et arrête mon émotion, ma participation, et bientôt va répondre tout autrement à mes précédentes interrogations.

Hémianopsie. Mais oui, c'était une hémianopsie qui m'arrivait, qui s'était glissée et subtilement jointe au spectacle! C'était d'elle les oscillations, les tremblements vibratoires plus prononcés à gauche qu'à droite... et l'ombre mystérieuse, profonde et vibrante, c'était d'elle.

La crise de migraine ophtalmique avait dû se déclencher à l'entrée de la salle, coïncidant avec les premières vues, provoquée par la lumière trop forte de l'éblouissant faisceau lumineux sur l'écran.

Les spasmes des petites artérioles cérébrales avaient fourni les vibrations d'apparence émotionnelle, l'oblitération partielle des corps,

their mistrust, they partly concealed themselves even as they marched.

Doubtless they had reason to be cautious, but their manner of walking was odd nevertheless. And yet not so very odd: this was theatre after all, and they were acting in such a way as to show themselves to be partisans who must, being what they are, keep out of sight and remain mysterious.

The astonishing film-maker, whose name I was longing to learn, had not only devised a method of disguise – one very suitable for conspirators who will practise concealment for as long as possible – he was the inventor of another trick too: by some new mechanical technique he caused a sort of sustained vibration to occur, something purely psychic conveyed through a means that was physical. Whatever it was, it gave the impression of life itself, of life in danger.

By rapid shifts, whose nature I could not define, and by a barely perceptible shaking, the apprehension men in danger feel and the alternating boldness and fear that plotters must experience before they act and launch a surprise attack, were admirably conveyed. Against such feelings the heart is quite defenceless.

I was more, far more than a spectator in that place. I felt forcibly attached, I was there with them, on the spot. I had never been so attached before. All I lacked was the power to touch them, and perhaps not even that. At times I drew back, their movements felt so real.

Never before had I felt so engaged by a performance, so present at it, so taken up into it.

It was a spectacular leap forward in my life as a spectator. All unawares I had entered the age to come. I marvelled aloud.

A sharp pain brings me suddenly to a halt, halts my emotion and my involvement, and before long answers my earlier questions in a quite different way.

Hemianopsia. That was what was happening to me, an attack, and subtly it had extended itself into the performance on the screen. Hence the oscillations and that trembling and vibrating more pronounced on the left than on the right... and the mysterious, deep and vibrating darkness, that too.

The migraine, affecting my vision, must have come on when I entered the hall, when my eyes first looked at the screen, and the light there, the brilliant concentration of light, must have been too strong for them and brought it on.

Spasms in the tiny cerebral arteries had given rise to vibrations of a seemingly emotional kind, and also to the partial obliteration

le «magique» des conspirateurs, leur surprenante dissimulation, leur angoisse si admirablement mimée, si physiquement approfondie. Le drame conjugué venait de mon propre tremblement, envahissement du scénique par le physiologique, confusion du spectacle et de l'atteinte visuelle du spectateur.

Le physique devenu psychique, il avait fallu cela pour obtenir cette justesse inouïe, autrement irréalisable.

Allons, l'époque nouvelle (quant au spectacle de film), il fallait la remettre à plus tard.

of the bodies, the conspirators' "magic", their astonishing powers of self-concealment and their wonderfully well acted fearfulness that was given such physical depth. The film and my own trembling were dramatically combined, the screen was invaded by my physiology, the spectator and the spectator's impaired vision were confused.

Physical become psychic: only thus (there could be no other way) had that unprecedented rightness been achieved.

As for the new era (in film, I mean), we shall have to wait.

Voyage qui tient à distance

Journey that keeps at a distance

Voyage qui n'en finissait pas, qui se tenait toujours à distance. C'était par une des journées les plus étouffantes d'un été oppressant. Ayant quitté, abattu, la capitale pour me rendre dans le Nord vers un peu de fraîcheur, je m'étais proposé de faire halte en chemin, auprès d'un ancien camarade condamné par une grave maladie à garder la chambre.

À l'intérieur d'un compartiment étouffant, longues sont les heures. Arrivant en retard, dans une température aussi chaude que celle que j'avais quittée le matin, je me trouve le soir, arrêté, non pas à la gare principale, mais à une station auxiliaire où je dois remonter dans un train local, bourré, bruyant et presque torride pour à la fin aboutir à la ville elle-même, à présent méconnaissable, son aspect moyenâgeux perdu dans de modernes constructions monotones.

Au lieu d'air frais, une atmosphère orageuse où stagne l'odeur écœurante et fade du pétrole, issue sans doute de raffineries installées dans une des boucles du fleuve. En ce port flamand, un récent comportement des habitants vis-à-vis du français, qu'ils feignent de ne plus comprendre, achève d'intercepter pour moi la ville familière d'autrefois.

De l'hôtel, sans monter à la chambre, je me rends à la nouvelle adresse où un appartement quelconque a remplacé le pavillon à l'ancienne où je le connus.

Je m'attendais à le trouver couché. Il vient à ma rencontre, le teint reposé, que j'envie, tandis qu'épuisé je voudrais tellement m'allonger. La conversation n'enlève pas ma fatigue, qu'il serait malséant et ridicule de mentionner, mais qui s'accroît, me met au bord de l'étourdissement, si bien que refusant des offres insistantes de passer la soirée ensemble, je prends congé précipitamment, non sans mauvaise conscience et avec de vagues promesses de revenir.

Je médite de me restaurer dans un endroit calme de ma connaissance où je n'aurai pas à parler.

Un échec de plus: restaurant fermé. À jeun, défait, je gagne ma chambre, désagréable, puritaine, à un seizième où dix-huitième étage où je me couche sans tarder.

La nuit déjà avancée, mon demi-sommeil se trouve interrompu à un moment comme par une injonction, et moi-même condamné, dirait-on.

Une sorte de signe me le fait entendre, et que... ce serait (?) de ma faute, à cause de quelque chose qui ne serait plus à sa place.

A journey that would not end, that kept itself for ever at a distance. A day in summer, one of the most stifling days in an oppressive summer. Flattened by the heat I had left the capital and was heading north for some fresh air. I thought I would break my journey and visit an old friend who was confined to his room by a serious illness.

Time passes very slowly in a stifling compartment. Arriving late, in temperatures as high as they were when I set off in the morning, I found myself deposited that evening not at the main station but at a smaller one some way out and obliged to continue in a local train, which was crammed, noisy and infernally hot but which brought me at last into the city itself, now unrecognisable, its medieval appearance lost among uniform modern buildings.

The air, instead of being fresh, was thundery and in it had settled the stale and sickly smell of oil, no doubt from the refineries that had been built in one of the loops of the river. The inhabitants of this Flemish port, having recently changed their attitude towards the French language, now pretend not to understand it, which completes my estrangement from the town I once knew well.

I leave the hotel without going up to my room and make my way to his new address. He had a nice old house when I first knew him; now he lives in a nondescript apartment.

I expected to find him in bed, but he comes out to meet me, he looks rested, which I envy him. I am exhausted and would give anything to lie down. The conversation fails to dispel my fatigue, which it would be churlish and absurd to mention but which grows until I am all but stupefied, and I refuse his very pressing invitations to spend the evening together and abruptly take my leave, feeling guilty and vaguely promising to come again.

My plan is to go somewhere quiet, to eat – a place I remember where I shan't need to talk.

Another failure: the restaurant is closed. Hungry, beaten, I return to my room, my austere and unpleasant room on the sixteenth or eighteenth floor, and go to bed at once.

Late in the night I am woken out of an uncertain sleep by something like a command. I feel condemned.

This is brought home to me by a sort of sign... and that I am perhaps culpable, because of something which has been displaced.

Il est trois heures du matin, mauvaise heure des mauvaises nuits. J'ouvre une des fenêtres dont j'écarte les volets. Je n'arrive pas à m'orienter. L'air entre mollement, chaud et lourd.

Rue étroite. Le regard plonge dans une profonde fosse noire que je ne peux considérer sans vertige. De l'étage élevé dont je fais partie, je surplombe la maison basse d'en face qui, toit défoncé, volets arrachés et fenêtres brisées, semble abandonnée. Noire, d'un noir qui ne signifie pas seulement absence de lumière, mais branchement retiré; on dirait un bâtiment dévalisé, saccagé... condamné.

Pièces que je me représente nues, comme ce qui resterait d'une maison pillée, bombardée. La ville l'a été en effet et assiégée, mais il y a bien trente ans, lors de la dernière guerre.

Se peut-il qu'on ait laissé ces maisons à l'abandon, ni entièrement détruites, ni reconstruites? En voie de démolition?

Spectacle malsain, misérable, partie de rue, pareille à ma journée, autre épave, à quoi elle se trouve amarrée. Et moi d'une certaine façon condamné aussi, comme mauvais ami peut-être, une fois de plus coupable d'indifférence.

Enfin je ferme la fenêtre et vais ouvrir l'autre qui à tout le moins ne donne pas sur cette étroite, démoralisante rue.

Un extraordinaire spectacle lumineux s'y présente, large, ample, éclairé a giorno sans raison visible.

Follement, éperdument flamboyant comme pour répondre aux besoins d'une circulation intense, mais où ne passe même pas un chien, un très large boulevard, éclairé, avec ostentation, dans le goût des habitants de ce port nordique, un des plus grands du monde dont ils ne sont pas peu fiers.

...attendant, dirait-on, le regard du voyeur.

Autant la rue à l'autre fenêtre est éteinte, morne, morte, maudite, autant l'artère large qui s'étale devant moi, claire à meurtrir l'œil, est illuminée comme pour des défilés ou pour une réception d'honneur... à cette heure où l'on ne voit pas un passant.

De loin en loin à toute allure, sans s'arrêter, sans ralentir, semblables à des estafettes attendues impérativement à l'autre bout de la ville, passent de puissantes autos strictement fermées.

Semblable à un espace scénique, mais pourtant tout ce qu'il y a de plus concret et vrai, cette ensorcelante étendue citadine, à l'air factice – nouveau choc, nouveau dérèglement de ma journée décidément difficile à redresser, à remettre au réel – jette pour rien ces

It is three in the morning, a bad time in a bad night.

I open one of the windows and push back the shutters. I can't get my bearings. The air is warm and heavy, it enters listlessly.

A narrow street. I look down into a deep black pit. Looking makes me giddy. From where I am, high up, I overhang the low house opposite. Its roof is stove in, its shutters have been ripped off, windows broken, it looks empty. The dark in that house is worse than mere absence of light: it is the dark when the supply has gone. The place looks broken into, ransacked, condemned.

I think of the rooms as bare, as what would be left of a house that has been bombed and pillaged. In fact that happened to the town, it was besieged, but more than thirty years ago, during the last war.

Could the houses have been abandoned as they are now, neither wholly destroyed nor ever rebuilt? In the process of being demolished?

It is a wretched and unwholesome sight, this bit of the street, and it resembles the sort of day I've had, a wreck of a day, the street and my wreck of a day are bound together. I am condemned in a certain sense myself, as a bad friend perhaps, guilty yet again of a lack of warmth.

Eventually I shut the window, cross to the other one and open that. It does not look over the narrow and dispiriting street at least.

Here what confronts me is an extraordinary brightness, a scene of great breadth and depth, lit up for no apparent reason as clear as daylight.

A very wide boulevard, absurdly, insanely illuminated as though to serve an immense amount of traffic, but nothing is stirring, not even a dog, a great show of light, in the ostentatious style of this northern port, which is one of the largest in the world, as its citizens like to boast.

...waiting, you might say, for the eyes of a voyeur.

As lightless, dismal, dead and cursed as is the street at the other window, to that same degree the wide thoroughfare before me here is lit, with a brightness that hurts the eyes, lit up as though for processions or a great reception... at an hour when not one passer-by is to be seen.

Very occasionally powerful cars come by. Their blinds are drawn, they never stop, they never slow down. They pass like messengers awaited with impatience on the other side of town.

Like a stage set, and yet as real and concrete as can be, this magical and seemingly artificial cityscape flings forth gratuitously, like a yelping noise, its harsh and excessive brightness, and forms with the narrow street that adjoins it (though invisible from here) a dual

brillances excessives, comme des glapissements, des stridences, et forme avec l'étroite rue qui y est attenante (mais qu'on n'aperçoit pas de cette fenêtre) un incroyable spectacle double, qu'on croirait plutôt onirique, ensemble irréel, impossible à accepter.

Faux boulevard, avec son vain air définitif, placé là, dirait-on, pour une nuit unique. Bloc de ville isolé, brillamment préparé pour quelque revue, mais sans habitants (détruits, absents, tous absents?). Ou mise en scène pour une pièce inconnue, prête à être jouée, que dans d'invisibles coulisses déjà des acteurs aidés d'ingénieurs et de techniciens répéteraient sans parole, sans discours... faux carrefour qui s'apparente à ma journée sans «prise».

Côté rue morte, lorsque après l'éblouissant boulevard je reviens à la première fenêtre et me retrouve sans transition par-dessus la noire maison en ruine d'en face, celle-ci paraît sortir d'un autre âge, pas lointain, décalé quand même, partie impossible à remboîter dans l'autre.

La lune entre-temps sur ces bâtiments délabrés s'est levée, exagérée, rouge, inadmissible, elle aussi, lune comme un énorme œil de cyclope en transe, et quant à la taille, semblable au plus grand soleil qu'on puisse voir au crépuscule dans les campagnes, lune souffrante et mauvaise qui pèse sur la ville, sur cette partie du moins, surveillant son appauvrissement, sa disparition progressive.

Mauvaise, insupportable surveillance.

Situation bizarrement dérangeante, qui avec deux segments de ville, toujours impossibles à unir et différemment privés d'habitants, de vie et de naturel, ne peuvent absolument pas arriver à faire un ensemble et, à ma fatigue, à mon vertige restent accrochés, fragments colossaux dépareillés dont je ne sais que faire... et dont je ne saurais à qui parler dans cette ville étrangère.

L'hôtel, grande tour élevée, anormalement silencieuse, son insonorisation outrée fait qu'on la ressent presque comme une tombe, une tombe démesurée, autre invraisemblance! Là encore la réalité m'est retirée. Ne va-t-elle plus revenir? N'y aurai-je plus droit? Ce serait absurde. L'idée pourtant se maintient.

...

Lentement va le temps. Un monceau de temps encore à passer avant le lever du jour.

... À l'intérieur d'une chambre sinistre, couleur de bagne, mais vertigineuse dès que je me penche au-dehors, tantôt rouvrant l'une ou l'autre fenêtre, tantôt me recouchant, inutilement fermant les yeux, pour du repos qui ne vient pas, je reste dans un état de non-défense.

60

phenomenon that surpasses belief, something dreamlike, an unreal entity impossible to credit. This is another shock, which further disturbs a day already hard enough to rectify and bring back to reality.

A false boulevard, unconvincing despite its appearance of permanence. It might have been put there just for the night A portion of the town cut off from all the rest, made ready, in brilliant style, for some great spectacle, but without its citizens (killed off, perhaps, or absent, all absent?). Or the set for an unknown play about to be staged, and in the invisible wings (engineers and technicians assisting them) the actors are ready to play their wordless, speechless parts... a false crossroads resembling the day I have spent, a day without "hold".

On the dead street side, when I leave the dazzling boulevard and find myself, with no transition, at the first window again above the house opposite, that black ruin seems to be emerging from a different age, not a distant age but one out of line and impossible to fit back into the other.

Meanwhile the moon has risen over these dilapidated structures, a gross red moon as hard to accept as the scene itslf, like the enormous eye of a furious cyclops, as big as the biggest sun you ever see at dusk in the open country, an ailing and baleful moon that weighs on the town, on this part at least, surveying its impoverishment and gradual disappearance.

Baleful, unbearable scrutiny.

It is queer and unsettling. The two parts of the town, for ever impossible to bring together, each in its own way destitute of inhabitants, life and naturalness, can never be made into an entity, absolutely not, and they remain as two odd and colossal fragments clinging to my fatigue and dizziness, defeating me... and to whom can I ever speak of them in this strange town?

The hotel rises to a towering height, abnormally silent, so soundproofed it feels like a tomb, like a vast tomb, and in that aspect too I am confronted by something hard to believe. There too reality has withdrawn from me. Never to return? Perhaps I shall never again have a right to reality? The idea is absurd, but I cannot dislodge it.

...

Slow passage of time. Still a little mountain of time must trickle away before dawn.

... In that sinister room, painted like a cell but vertiginous if I look out, I offer no defence. I open one of the windows, then the other. Or I lie down again and close my eyes, to sleep, but sleep eludes me.

À quoi tient la réalité! À quoi tient une ville! À quoi tient aussi un remords! Je le vois, rien comme un remords pour miner, désagréger.

On voudrait, impuissant, que ce qui fut n'ait pas été. On revient sans cesse à ce mur achevé du passé, qui serait à réaliser autrement, mais qui ne part pas, et seulement trouble les alentours qui obtusément s'y irréalisent, en vous défaisant vous-même.

. . . .

Le lendemain, à la première heure, sans prendre des nouvelles de qui que ce soit, je filai comme un voleur par le premier train en partance vers la frontière du Nord. Là, d'innombrables canaux et maisons si différentes comme aussi l'habillement et l'allure des habitants, appelant l'attention vers d'autres dehors, se structurèrent pour composer un peuple, un pays... se substituant de la sorte à la grande ville borgne d'hier.

Ma mauvaise conscience non plus ne pouvait suivre. L'autre, l'habituelle le pouvait. Son tour était revenu.

J'avais une dernière fois quitté le pays des porte-à-faux.

Le temps aussi était plus froid.

What *is* reality? What is a city? And another thing: what is re-morse? It becomes clear to me that there is nothing so undermin-ing and disintegrating as remorse.

Helplessly wishing that what is were not. Again and again coming back to the finished wall of the past that ought to be other than it is but it stays and queers everything around it, against that wall every-thing stupidly becomes unreal and in the process undoes you as well.

. . . .

Next morning, at first light, without contacting anyone whatso-ever, I left like a thief on the first train that would take me to the northern frontier. There the innumerable canals and the very dif-ferent houses and the clothing and the bearing of the inhabitants, all drawing my attention to other exteriors, took shape and composed a people and a country... and so replaced the unsavoury city of the night before.

Likewise my bad conscience was left behind. But the conscience I usually have came with me. I reinstated it.

For the last time I had left the land where things are out of true.

The weather was cooler too.

Musique en déroute

Music in disarray

J'acquis un jour un petit instrument de musique africain, petit même dans sa catégorie, tenant aisément dans la main.

Sur une mince palette d'un beau bois brun sombre, dix lamelles de fer. Il en manquait une, peut-être deux. Vieilles, ébréchées, mal forgées, les survivantes étaient aussi mal insérées.

J'étais à cette époque simplement en quête d'une sanzas, instrument au son discret, incapable de troubler et même d'atteindre l'oreille d'un voisin.

Au premier son qui sortit de celui-ci, il fut reconnu hors d'usage. Je le pris néanmoins. Des années passèrent.

Un jour de dégoût de tout, étant, après un accident, immobilisé, étendu sans repos, pied plâtré, impotent, un matin donc, plus vide qu'un autre, le propre à rien que j'étais redevenu songeait lourdement.

Sur l'horizon de mes possibilités réduites, dans le vague je cherchais, quand mes regards rôdant de tous côtés rencontrèrent ce vieil objet mal en point, acquisition de mauvaise mémoire.

L'humeur sombre j'attrapai ce bancal, bancal comme moi. Dans la demi-obscurité de ce matin d'hiver en ma chambre étroite et quasi sans le regarder, je laissai tomber sur lui un doigt, sans dessein particulier. Sur-le-champ il répondit.

Depuis peut-être quinze ans, non, trente au moins, il était là, ne révélant pas son secret.

Le petit instrument dédaigné venait de répondre. Il ne lui avait manqué jusque-là pour le faire réagir que de la brusquerie, du dégoût, un rageur découragement qu'à présent je pouvais lui apporter en abondance.

Il n'émit d'abord qu'un cra-cra comme eût fait un vieux corbeau cynique, le moins dupe des oiseaux, le plus impitoyable, qui jamais ne laissera sans l'achever l'être vivant petit ou grand qu'il découvre momentanément incapable de défense.

Cependant je faisais à l'instrument répéter et répéter le signal de désolation, ce son dévastateur pour moi sauveur, l'expression têtue du «sans espoir», je l'écoutais avec avidité.

Pas de discours. Pas d'enchaînement. Seulement dénégation sur dénégation. Un unique son rébarbatif. Il suffisait.

Rien pour *chanter*, tout pour maltraiter chant et enchantement. Refus, refus d'emblée, brutalisant la complaisance toujours là, la

One day I acquired a musical instrument from Africa. It was small even of its kind, and easily fitted into the hand.

It had ten little iron tongues on a slim board of beautiful dark brown wood. One or two more were missing, and those it had were old, chipped, badly forged and even badly inserted.

At the time I was simply looking for a sansa. They don't make a loud noise – not so the neighbours would be disturbed or even hear it.

I knew as soon as I heard this one that it was useless. I took it nevertheless. Years passed.

One day then, sick of everything, laid up after an accident with my foot in plaster, laid out unable to move and unable to rest, on a morning more vacant even than usual, useless again and stupid in my thoughts,

I was scouting the horizon of my reduced possibilities, prowling vaguely this side and that, when my eyes lit upon the battered old sansa, my unhappy purchase.

I took it up. In my gloomy mood we seemed two of a kind: both brokendown. A winter morning, my cramped room was in semi-darkness. I fingered the instrument with scarcely a glance at it and with no particular intention. At once it responded.

For perhaps fifteen years, no, for thirty at least, it had lain there, keeping its secret.

Now the despised little instrument had responded. All it had wanted, to make it react, was brusqueness, spleen, bad temper and despondency, which in my present mood I was able to bring to it in abundance.

What it gave out at first was a cawing noise, like a crow, a cynical old crow whom nothing fools or moves to pity but anything he finds defenceless for a moment, large or small, any living thing, he never lets go and finishes it off.

Meanwhile I was making the instrument repeat and repeat again its desolating call. The ruin it expressed, its obstinate utterance of hopelessness, gave me release. I listened with a sort of greed.

It was not discourse. Nothing was joined. It was simply denial upon denial. One single harsh and hostile note. And that sufficed.

There was nothing in this of *singing*, everything in it did violence to song and the magic of song. Refusal, flat refusal, a brutal rejec-

concession qui presque fatalement vient avec le prolongement, avec la composition.

Brusque le son faisait sans effort revenir à ma mémoire les corbeaux au vol lent qui apparaissent, précédés de leur criaillement lugubre près des falaises ou dans la campagne par temps venteux, lorsque les branches geignent ou cassent et que ces oiseaux de malheur au funèbre appareil phonateur lancent, de façon à semer la panique où ils passent, leur cri insistant. Que les oisillons tombés du nid et les bêtes blessées gisant par terre perdent toute illusion sur l'avenir. Sinistre est la menace d'en haut.

Imagination mise à part, le son que je continuais à susciter était un son cassé, qui ne pouvait se montrer que cassé. D'abord vibrant fortement, puis vivement écourté, comme venant d'un ressort qui se rompt, qui ne peut plus vibrer davantage. L'impression venait qu'il s'y refusait, la musicalisation semblait repoussée «exprès».
Ainsi recommençait à vivre l'antique *sanzas*.

Combien d'êtres désolés, ou furieux, me disais-je, combien d'esclaves désemparés sur le continent noir, s'étaient déjà confrontés avec elle, causant à la longue le brillant de l'extrémité des lames d'où leurs doigts errants en avaient tiré une désolation où ils se reconnaissaient.
Le vieil instrument dérangé pouvait rendre cela, comme aucune formation orchestrale ne l'aurait pu.
Le «criaillement» et tout était dit. Cette seule lamelle y suffisait. J'étais tombé sur celle-là rendant tout autre profération dérisoire. Psychothérapie parfaite, adaptée.

Après avoir expérimenté et repris quantité de fois cette sorte de déclaration antimusicale définitive, n'attendant plus rien au-delà, je décidai quand même de m'aventurer sur d'autres lamelles, qui ne devaient pas avoir été mises là sans raison.
J'en essaie une, puis une autre, toutes pour finir.
Chacune insuffisante va dans ma présente insuffisance pouvoir me servir et au-delà de mon attente.
Si petit que fût cet instrument c'était comme si j'en avais eu quatre dans la main, quatre instruments absolument différents (ou quatre débris), aussi différents qu'une viole l'est d'un tambour,

tion of the agreeableness which is always there, of the concessions almost inevitably made when notes are prolonged or put together in a composition.

The sound, so abrupt, naturally made me think of crows and their slow flight when they appear in windy weather around cliffs or in the country and their lugubrious cawing goes ahead of them and branches groan and break and those unlucky birds, equipped with the voice of death, reiterate their call, and panic spreads wherever they pass. Fledglings fallen from the nest and creatures lying hurt can abandon all illusions about the future. A sinister thing is threatening from above.

But setting aside whatever I might imagine, the sound I was continuing to produce was a broken sound, and could never come forth as anything other than broken. First came a strong vibration, then abruptly cut short, as though made by a spring, and the spring had broken and could not vibrate anymore. But the impression it gave was one of refusal, as though the possibility of making music were rejected "deliberately".

It was thus that the ancient *sansa* came back to life.

I wondered how many grieving or furious human beings, how many of black Africa's bewildered slaves had already encountered it and caused, at length, the tips of its tongues to shine, their moving fingers having brought forth from them the notes of a desolation in which they recognised their own.

The old and damaged instrument could utter that as no orchestra would ever have been able to.

The "cawing noise" said everything. The one tongue sufficed. I had chanced upon that one, and to try to add anything would have been ridiculous. As psychotherapy it was perfect. It suited.

Having then many times tried out that, so to speak, definitive statement against all music, and expecting nothing beyond it, I decided nevertheless to experiment with the other tongues, which were surely there for a purpose.

I tried one, then another, and finally all of them.

All being unsatisfactory and that being how I felt myself, they would serve me well and better than I had expected.

Small as the instrument was it was as if I had four of them in my hand, four absolutely different instruments (or four separate pieces), as different as a viola is from a drum – four, all capable of

sans relation l'un avec l'autre – quatre pour décourager n'importe quelle entreprise musicale. D'accord seulement pour intercepter, exclure toute mélodie parfaite. Opposés à tout... ensemble.

Quoi que je pusse entreprendre en cette funeste période devait rester dans l'ellipse et m'arrêtait. Si je m'obstinais, je culbutais invariablement sur une note d'un tout autre registre, d'une autre composition sonore. Ou bien dernier recours une lamelle mal cabrée bourdonnait et restait bourdonnante et dubitative.

Individualités pour séparer non pour unir. Pas du tout genre quatuor. Pas davantage faites pour l'ornement ou pour la virtuosité.

Aucun bon voisinage à attendre de ces perturbateurs.

J'avais enfin trouvé, et à portée de mes doigts, une sorte d'ensemble instrumental, l'«orchestre intempestif».

Sons orphelins, torchons musicaux. J'allais errant de l'un à l'autre.

. . . .

Pause. Longue pause. Des jours durant.

Est-ce que j'allais retrouver notre entente?

Malgré un désir particulier que j'avais de retourner à la connivence éprouvée, j'hésitais à y revenir.

Je n'avais plus, je ne pouvais plus avoir la magnifique révélation du début.

À tort j'étais inquiet. Cette petite sanzas de rien du tout avait encore bien des choses à m'enseigner.

D'emblée, toujours en dissidence, touchée par mes doigts, elle me lâcha une rafale de refus. Mécontentement n'avait pas diminué.

L'humeur batailleuse (notre conjointe humeur) avait plutôt augmenté.

De nouveaux essais eurent lieu, puis nouvel abandon. Après quelque temps, la sanzas se trouva bonne pour la divagation.

Différents troubles s'ajoutaient à la mise en déroute de toute composition organisée. La manquante échelle de sons s'entendait avec l'exécutant pour tout ce qui pouvait aller avec confiance, harmonie, espérance et raison. Il en sortait aussi de l'ubuesque.

L'esprit sardonique et brouillon fixé dans cet instrument, sûrement aucun gri-gri ne l'aurait pu empêcher. Il était maintenant trop tard. Une malfaisance d'incrédule, de révolté y était à demeure.

rendering hopeless any musical enterprise. They were united in one thing only: the thwarting and exclusion of any perfect melody. They were opposed to everything... together.

Whatever I undertook in that dismal time I was certain to fall back and come to a halt. If I persisted then, invariably, a note in a quite different register, belonging in some other sequence of sounds, would send me head over heels. Or else, one final trick, a badly set tongue would hum and remain humming and doubtful.

These were individualities made to put asunder and not to join. There was nothing of the quartet in them. Nor were they made for ornament or virtuosity.

There was no neighbourliness in these disturbers of the peace.

At last I had found, within reach of my fingers, a sort of instrumental ensemble, "the untimely band".

They were orphan sounds, musical rags. I wandered aimlessly among them.

. . . .

A pause. A long pause. Lasting for days.

Would I be able to revive our understanding?

Though I had a very particular desire to return to our proven complicity, I hesitated.

That first magnificent revelation had faded, inevitably.

I need not have worried. My unprepossessing little sansa still had a lot to teach me.

Still dissident, when I touched it again, at once it answered me with a volley of refusals. There was no diminution of discontent.

Indeed, the combative mood (the mood we shared) had, if anything, intensified.

There were fresh attempts. Then again it was put to one side. Later I found the sansa good for wandering in the mind.

My various troubles joined in the process of putting every organised music to flight. The player was in league with his instrument's deficient scale, in league against harmony, faith and hope and reason. Grotesque things came out too.

No amount of pleasantry could ever have subdued the sardonic and disruptive spirit of that instrument. It was too late. In it for ever lay the sceptic's and the malcontent's bad deeds.

Des lames dépareillées une surtout, brouillonne entre toutes, fer forgé eût-on dit par la malfaisance pour provoquer malfaisance et perturbation, faisait sensation.

Cette indépendante, je trouvais fascination à l'introduire parmi les voisines, chantantes (relativement).

D'une malfaisance souveraine et sans remède, elle recelait un «esprit mauvais», que peut-être un garnement en l'absence du forgeron, du patron, avait précipitamment forgée. De cet inventeur inconnu je recueillais médusé la trouvaille inattendue, fruit d'un essai sommaire.

Les cinq chantantes je les laissais un peu de côté, puisque insuffisantes pour composer un tissu musical délibéré dont seulement elles donnaient l'envie.

J'aimais surtout quand elles avaient paru aller avec telle ou telle des indépendantes qui aussitôt évidemment y faisait une brèche dont le «morceau» ne se remettait pas, et qui ne pouvait plus être comblée.

Et tout le superbe préparé tombait avec l'avenir envisagé.

Lorsque longtemps après je repris l'instrument pour en jouer, je ne le reconnus pas. Ce petit brutal, fait pour exprimer seulement «patatra», pour exécuter à chaque instant un tête-à-queue complet, coucou dans un nid de chardonnerets, lequel éjecte sans pitié les jeunes oisillons, trouvés au nid des vrais parents, n'en laissait plus rien paraître. Ce que j'entendais était tout différent et je ne l'aurais pas cru possible, surtout lorsque je tenais les yeux fermés, pour n'être que tout oreille. J'étais malmené ailleurs.

On aurait dit des bruits d'eau dans des gouttières, dans des canalisations, y tournant, y débouchant mais sans violence ni grande difficulté. Séquences certes toujours absentes, mais ayant cessé de déranger et d'être malvenues. Nous étions remis (!) (à quoi? à qui?). Il restait un instrument aux faibles moyens.

Pour créer mésentente ce n'était donc pas une languette dont je disposais, mais trois ou quatre des suivantes, qui à leur tour contaminées perdaient leurs possibilités dont n'apparaissait que le premier appel, jamais la suite.

Jusqu'au bout la musique de cet instrument était bien le contraire de l'habituellement recherché.

Contre l'attendrissement, contre sa banalisation surtout, si fréquents en musique, c'en était la mise en garde incorruptible.

The odd tongues were all disruptive, but one was outstandingly so. It astonished me: it seemed forged by wickedness itself to incite disturbances and further wickedness.

I liked bringing in this outsider among its (relatively speaking) melodious companions.

In its sovereign and incurable wickedness it seemed to harbour an "evil spirit" that perhaps had been fastened in there by some delinquent apprentice working hastily in the absence of the smith, his master. And I was now the horror-struck receiver of that unknown inventor's surprise, of the thing he had hastily created.

I left the five more tuneful tongues rather to one side since they were in fact incapable of composing any deliberate piece of music but only made me wish to.

I particularly enjoyed it when they seemed to go along with one or other of the outsiders: these at once, needless to say, caused a breach from which the "piece" was unable to recover and which could not thereafter be filled.

And everything proudly beginning collapsed at the sight of its future.

Much later, when I took up the instrument again, to play it, I no longer recognised it. The brutal little thing, made to emit nothing but sounds of disaster, to be always fundamentally contrary, to be the cuckoo in a nest of goldfinches mercilessly evicting the youngsters from their rightful home, showed no such character now. What I heard was quite different and I would not have believed it possible, especially not when I closed my eyes, to do nothing but listen. I was having a rough time elsewhere.

It sounded like water in gutters, in channels, turning and pouring forth, but without violence or any great difficulty. There was still, of course, a want of continuity; but this was no longer disturbing, no longer awkward. We were restored (!) (to what? to whom?). We were left with an instrument poor in means.

To produce dissension I had not *one* little tongue of metal at my disposal but three or four of those in sequence with it, which, becoming contaminated in their turn, lost their expressive possibilities and only gave out a beginning and never what should have followed.

To the last this instrument's music was quite the opposite of what we habitually seek.

It was on guard incorruptibly against sentiment and above all against the trivialising of sentiment, which are so common in music.

Hors série, il y avait encore un cri d'étranglé qui «va» crier, mais ne le peut, expression devant laquelle toute autre devenait artificielle.

Une des lames, anormalement rentrée, que le doigt trouvait difficulté à joindre, était la cause de ce son déserteur, poulie qui soudain lâche. Même en la malmenant, on ne pouvait l'amener à un autre effet qu'à ce cri étrange, aussitôt rentré, étouffé. Le cri du gamin désobéissant, pensai-je, son dernier cri lorsqu'on l'attrapa avec le produit de son larcin. C'est ce cri qu'on entendait, qu'on lui avait brutalement rentré dans la gorge... ensuite passé par magie dans le fer maudit.

Outside the series there was another sound: the cry of a man being strangled who is "about to" cry, but cannot; and confronted by expressiveness like that any other seemed artificial.

A tongue too far embedded, that the finger had trouble engaging, was the cause of this treacherous sound, the sound of a pulley when it suddenly lets go. No matter how one abused it, it could not be induced to make any response but that strange cry immediately withdrawn and stifled. The cry of a disobedient urchin, I thought, his last cry on being caught in possession of his theft. That was the cry I could hear, a cry brutally forced back down the boy's throat... and by sorcery afterwards transmitted into this cursed steel.

Où poser la tête?

Where to lay the head?

Paresse

Paresse: rêve sans fin qui rêve indérangée
la vie, parenthèse fluide

Alentour, projets, plans, départs,
Des édifices tombent, montent, remontent,

Paresse rêve
sur son puits qui s'approfondit

Plaines où l'on plane

Plaines
par-dessus de hautes plaines de nuages
on plane
on plane
où l'on planerait toute la vie

La terre pour finir revient faiblement
basse, bâtie, trop bâtie, aplatie
large tapis parcouru de haut, de très haut,

vers d'impérieux tracés en longues lignes.
La grande aile, où l'on est, vire
... se pose

Retour, réseaux, couloirs... l'air si fade
taupes obscures rentrant dans l'obscur

Idleness

Idleness: dream without end that dreams life
underanged, a fluid parenthesis

Around, projects, plans, departures,
Buildings fall, they rise, they rise up again,

Idleness dreams
over its deepening well

Plains in another plane

Plains
above plateaux of clouds
gliding
gliding
we could spend our lives there gliding

Faintly, to finish, back comes the earth
low, with its building, too much building, the flattened earth
high, very high, we skim it like a widespread carpet

down to the long lines of the commanding routes.
The great wing, where we are, tilts
... and lands.

Homecoming, networks, corridors... the air so insipid
obscure moles re-entering obscurity

Situation-torse

Torse sans tête, adieu à la tête, cette comparse
qui toujours interfère
De sourires qui épient, le torse se passe
de paroles, ficelles qui nouent,
renouent
retiennent

Complet sans explication, le torse
à l'égal d'un Pharaon
Qui peut dépouiller un torse?

Des ensembles à présent...

On voit passer des torses

Torso situation

Headless torso, goodbye head, a supernumerary
forever interfering
The torso does without smiles (they spy)
and words (being strings that knot
and knot again
and fasten)

The torso, complete without explanation
Pharaoh's equal
Who can fleece a torso?

Entireties now...

We see torsos passing by

Où poser la tête?

Un ciel
un ciel parce qu'il n'y a plus la terre,
sans une aile, sans un duvet, sans une plume d'oiseau, sans une buée

strictement, uniquement ciel
un ciel parce qu'il n'y a plus la terre

Après le coup de grisou dans la tête, l'horreur, le désespoir
après qu'il n'y a plus rien eu, tout dévasté, sabordé, toute issue
    perdue

un ciel glacialement ciel

Obstrué à présent, barré, bourré de débris;
ciel à cause de la migraine de la terre
dépourvue de ciel

un ciel parce qu'il n'y a plus nulle part où poser la tête

Traversé, rétréci, rentré, rogné, défait intermittent, irrespirable dans
    les explosions et les fumées
bon à rien

un ciel désormais irretrouvable

Where to lay the head?

A sky
a sky because earth no longer is
not a wing, neither down nor the feather of a bird, not a wisp

strictly and only sky
a sky because the earth no longer is

After the blast in the head, the horror, the hopelessness
after there was nothing anymore but everything waste, scuttled
and every exit lost

a sky glacially sky

Obstructed at present, blocked and full of debris;
sky because of the migraine of the earth
deprived of sky

a sky because now there is nowhere to lay the head

Traversed, shrunk, withdrawn, eaten away, here and there undone,
    unbreathable in the explosions and the smoke
good for nothing

a sky henceforth never to be found again

Dictées

Penchées
Têtes appliquées
Aucune ne se relève
La dictée ne le permet pas

Les enseignements s'ajoutent aux ans
Des mouvements sont ressentis
des actes parfois suivent des sortes de certitude

Insistants attraits: réponses à une dictée
inscrite en chacun, en petit, en tout petit

Ça ne les gêne pas d'obéir à une dictée?

Autrefois, dans sa grandeur
l'Immense aux noms sacrés...

Restée seule, menue, tenace
traversant les ans, les rides,
la sourde dictée continue, en silence toujours

les infimes dieux incorporés commandent sans parler

Dictations

Bowed
Concentrating heads
Not one looks up
Dictation does not allow it

Lessons are added to the years
Movements felt
acts sometimes follow kinds of certitude

Insistent attractions: replies to a dictation
inscribed in everyone, written small, very small

They don't mind obeying a dictation?

Formerly, in grandeur
Immensity with holy names...

Left alone, slight, tenacious
crossing the years, the wrinkles,
the muffled dictation continues always in silence

the lowly incorporated gods give orders without speaking

Sans pli, sans repli, sûr de lui,
regards aux dents de loup
sous ses sourcils noirs comme entre des meurtrières
le prophète envahisseur – paraclet aux cent pouvoirs
commandant aux innocents aux sourcils faibles
fait accourir l'Avenir
créant rumeurs, créant tumeurs, –
Le dégageant des événements, de l'inertie, du quotidien
poussant l'idée utopique, vrille incontrôlée
sous les fronts des naïfs
où elle s'enfonce sans résistance.

Prison ensuite, le Pouvoir s'étant inquiété.
Oubli. Disparition.
Mais l'*idée*, à nouveau là, sous d'autres noms
revenue à l'époque suivante,
à celle qui lui était destinée
et l'attendait sans le savoir,
cette fois tout envahit, irrésistible.

*

Unruffled, unmoving, sure of himself,
eyes like the teeth of a wolf
eyes under their black brows like loopholes
the invading prophet – the comforter whose powers are legion
lord of the innocents whose brows are negligible
he calls up The Future
creating rumours and tumours, –
He releases it from events, from inertia, from the everyday
he pushes the idea of utopia, like a drill, unchecked,
it confronts the simplehearted
and enters them unopposed.

Prison then, Power having been alarmed.
He is forgotten. Disappears.
But the *idea*, present again, under other names
returns to the following age,
the one it was destined for
the one that was waiting without knowing,
and this time invades everything irresistibly.

*

De loin, de partout en groupes ils viennent
pour des palais, des monuments,
pour admirer.

À part sur le pavé, un homme simple arrêté
à ses pieds une mare
dans le fini des villes, infini hasard.

Après la grande, la toute grande destruction à venir
après l'appauvrissement partout, l'anéantissement
il restera toujours des mares

*

Des bras dans tous les sens
Ils lui reviennent

À l'homme quelconque,
au démuni que nul ne remarque
à l'insignifiant

dans ses moments d'épuisement
ils lui sont revenus.

Il ne sent plus tellement de besoins à présent
avec tant de bras.

dans l'espace, en mouvements
en tout sens.

*

From afar, from everywhere, they arrive in parties
for palaces and monuments
with their admiration.

But a simple man has halted on the street alone
a puddle at his feet
infinite chance in the finiteness of cities.

After the great, the supremely great destruction which is to come
after the coming of poverty everywhere and extinction
there will still be puddles

*

Arms in all directions
They are coming back to him

To nobody in particular,
to a man deprived whom nobody notices
to one of no importance

in his moments of exhaustion
they have come back to him.

His needs are fewer now
with so many arms.

in space, in movements
in every sense.

*

Après des ans
des ans comme des jours
l'examen d'admission reprend

Le Gouverneur après ce temps
nouvelle cérémonie est élu commis,
valet ensuite
à présent reçu balayeur

Ainsi de rang en rang abaissé
un jour sera retrouvé aux étables, à la porcherie

Descendra-t-il plus bas?
On l'y portera...

*

After a lapse of years
years like days
the entrance examination is resumed

The Governor, after this lapse of time,
in a new ceremony is elected clerk,
then valet
and admitted now as a roadsweeper

Descending rank by rank
one day he will be found in the stables, in the sty

Will he go further down?
He will be carried down...

*

Le temps le plus propice pour naître
n'était pas
n'est pas aujourd'hui

La Tour de la Mort s'élève
se voit déjà de partout
n'aura pas sa pareille

En un cercle, un cercle immensément large
des cycles s'achèvent
Des victimes sans tarder, seront là, présentes.
Simultanéité toujours si remarquable
des sacrifiés et des armés.

*

The best time to be born
was not
is not today

The Tower of Death has arisen
is already visible everywhere
will be without equal

In a circle, an immensely large circle
cycles are finishing
Victims soon will present themselves.
That always remarkable coming together
of the sacrificed and the bearers of arms.

*

Ils comparent
Sans cesse comparent

Mal composent
Davantage se décomposent
soudain parfois en ailes de moulins se recomposent
puis menhirs, sans plus bouger.

Espaces lacunaires

Une truie énorme occupe un grand bassin
approchée par beaucoup
Rumeurs toujours alentour
n'a pas été délogée encore.

L'éloignement des étoiles a fait baisser les têtes.

*

They compare
Ceaselessly compare

Badly compose
And decompose all the worse
suddenly sometimes recompose as windmill wings
then menhirs, never ever moving.

Gaps in spaces

An enormous sow inhabits a good-sized cistern
and many have approached her
Always rumours all around
still has not been evicted.

The stars are so far off we have bowed our heads.

*

Sur étrave

Sur une haute étrave fendant une mer sans flot
un être debout penché sur l'avant

Passent obliquement d'autres étraves
leur occupant pareillement penché

Pas de port. Ports inconnus

Quelques signes parfois d'étrave à étrave
qui alors se rapprochent.

At the prow

On a high prow cleaving a level sea
a figure standing inclined over the bowsprit

Obliquely other prows pass
their occupants inclining similarly

No port. Ports are unknown

Signs occasionally from prow to prow
which then approach.

Essais d'enfants
Dessins d'enfants

Children's ventures
Children's drawings

A

L'enfant à qui on fait tenir dans sa main un morceau de craie va sur la feuille de papier tracer désordonnément des lignes encerclantes, les unes presque sur les autres.

Plein d'allant, il en fait, en refait, ne s'arrête plus.

. . . .

En tournantes, tournantes lignes de larges cercles maladroits,
emmêlés,
incessamment repris
encore, encore
comme on joue à la toupie

Cercles. Désirs de la circularité.
Place au tournoiement

Au commencement est la
RÉPÉTITION

Emprise
seuls les cercles font le tour
le tour d'on ne sait quoi
de tout
du connu, de l'inconnu qui passe
qui vient, qui est venu,
et va revenir

Circulantes lignes de la démangeaison d'inclure
(de comprendre? de tenir? de retenir?)

Fouillis finalement
fibrilles fouillis fourmillant

. . . .

A

A child given paper and a piece of crayon will begin chaotically drawing lines – lines that make circles, almost on top of each other.

Off he goes, he draws circles and more circles, on and on.

. . . .

Lines turning and turning in wide clumsy circles,
entangled,
beginning again and again
and again
like spinning a top

Circles. The wish for circularity.
Make way for whirling

In the beginning is
REPETITION

Ascendancy
only circles do the round
the round of who knows what
of it all
of the known, of the unknown passing
that comes, has come,
and will come again

Circling lines of the urge to include
(comprehend? hold? keep?)

Finally a tangle
fibrils a tangle in a ferment

. . . .

C'est l'âge où l'enfant ressent pour tout ce qui tourne un plaisir sans pareil, où rien n'est plus désiré que de chevaucher des chevaux de bois qui tournent, en s'élevant et s'abaissant rythmiquement, l'âge où quasi magique est le cerceau, le ballon.

À présent de lui-même avec ses propres forces... le petit d'homme va faire s'accomplir des tours, de façon à en voir, à en retenir la trace. Mais plus que les traces, le geste compte, l'acte, le «faire» du cercle.

En quelle période plus que dans la première enfance est ressenti le circulaire, ce qui fait le tour, lequel comprend départ et retour.

Risque et joie du départ. Besoin du retour ensuite.

L'aller et le retour, le cercle, forme à la fois de l'élan et du refuge (l'enfant n'étant pas encore libéré de l'appréhension d'être un jour perdu, hors du milieu de la famille qu'il ne pourrait plus retrouver).

... Première et inconsciente abstraction, le cercle et combien vaste et combien de fois différemment se présentant, la vie même, la vie dans la vie.

Cercle, ce qui est mitoyen du dehors et du dedans, du pensable et de l'imaginable. Et du perçu et du retenu, de tout ce qui confusément encore devra être inclus.

Et vient l'ivresse, de toutes la plus naturelle, l'ivresse de la répétition, première des drogues.

Retour, retour, retour à n'en plus finir.

Les cercles parfaits des dessinateurs et des géomètres n'intéressent pas l'enfant. Les cercles imparfaits de l'enfant n'intéressent pas l'adulte. Il les appelle gribouillis, n'y voit pas le principal, l'élan, le geste, le parcours, la découverte, la reproduction exaltante de l'événement circulaire où une main encore faible, inexpérimentée, s'affermit.

Un stade des traits, lignes tracées à tort et à travers, peut aussi prendre place au début, joie gestuelle désordonnée.

Un jour, un jour après beaucoup de jours, échappant à la ronde bachique, une ligne incurvée ne fera pas le tour attendu: voici qu'elle ralentit et va s'arrêter, une certaine ligne à l'enfant surpris, ça lui dit quelque chose, le tient en suspens et le fait se retenir et considérer...

102

At that age the child takes a boundless delight in everything that revolves, wants nothing so much as to sit astride the wooden horses that revolve with a rhythmical rising and falling, at that age the hoop and the balloon are almost magical.

Now of his own accord with his own resources... the human infant will make circuits happen, to see the line they take and to retain it. But more than the line it is the gesture itself that counts, the act, the "doing" of the circle.

At no time more than in early childhood is there so strong a sense of what is circular, of things that make a circuit, in which are contained departure and return.

The risk and the joy of departure. The need to come back again.

Going and coming back, the circle, which is the shape both of the surging forward and of being safe (since the child is not yet free of the fear of being lost one day outside the family's centre and of never finding it again).

... The circle is the first unthinking abstraction, and however vast and however many guises it appears in it is life itself, life within life.

A circle is that which runs between outside and in, between the thinkable and the imaginable. And between what has been perceived and what has been retained, it runs through the confusion of things still waiting to be included.

And it intoxicates, in the most natural way of all, through repetition, our first drug.

Returning, returning, returning without end.

The perfect circles of draughtsmen and geometricians do not interest the child. The imperfect circles of children do not interest adults. They call them scribbles, miss the point, which is their energy, the gesture, the journey, discovery, the excited reproduction of a circular event in which a hand still lacking in strength, still inexperienced, asserts itself.

At the start there may also be a phase of drawing lines – lines all over the place – of gestures made for the love of it, wildly.

One day, one day after many days, a curving line will escape from the bacchic round and fail to complete the circuit expected of it: a particular line, surprising the child, it slows and halts, it says something to him, keeps him in suspense, makes him hold back and begin to think...

La trace linéaire laissée sur le papier lui rappelle quelqu'un, la mère, ou le père, l'homme déjà, l'homme représentant tous les hommes, l'homme même.

Fermée complètement ou incomplètement, la forme incurvée, que maintenant l'enfant voit venir de loin, va l'attirer de plus en plus. L'homme, c'est trouvé pour toujours. Il s'en est emparé et va en faire tant et plus. Il en est sûr.

Confiant, aussitôt «croyant» d'une exaltante croyance, il se prépare à les revoir, à les retrouver dans ses lignes, à les y faire revenir, de plus en plus les rappelant, de plus en plus aisément.

La tête déjà est importante. Dominante, grosse autant et plus que le corps, lequel n'offre rien de particulier, tandis que la tête (qui dans la réalité sait déjà accomplir tant de fonctions, manger, sucer, mordre, voir, entendre, goûter, retirer, embrasser, gazouiller, crier, rire, grimacer, faire peur, faire enrager, parler peut-être), la tête est dans son dessin la maîtresse partie, accapareuse entre toutes les parties corporelles.

Au début, âge de la tête (surprenant savoir prophétique!). Et simultanément une vraie vue d'embryologiste: comme chez tous les embryons de mammifères, la tête de l'embryon humain est incroyablement grosse...

La tête seule est pour lui indispensable.

Une tête rencontre une tête, tandis que les pieds – simple accompagnement – peuvent manquer et le genou et le cou et le reste qui viendront plus tard. Sur le moment il n'y revient pas. L'âge des retouches n'est pas arrivé.

En ses dessins il ne copie pas l'homme; il le campe. Événement de la ressemblance, fût-elle la plus gauche. L'analogie, il y est, enfant transporté de joie, sur la voie dont il ne découvre encore que le premier tronçon, l'essentiel qui, en quantité d'opérations de l'esprit, reviendra.
Premier accueil. Simplicité.

Informe, pauvrement formé, encore sans bras, le corps, et sans attaches les bras, sortis du cou, de n'importe où, de la tête, de la

The line left on the page reminds him of someone, his mother or his father, or even man, a man representing all men, man himself.

This curved shape, either closed or not quite closed, that now the child sees approaching from a distance, this shape will attract him more and more. Man once found is found for ever. He has seized hold of him and vigorously will do the same again. He is sure of him.

He has confidence, he is at once a believer with an exalted belief, he makes ready to see his figures again, to find them again in his lines, to make them come back there, summoning them more and more, ever more easily.

The head is already important. It dominates, it is at least as large as the body, which has no special features, whereas the head (which in real life is already able to do so many things: eat, suck, bite, see, hear, taste, withdraw, kiss, babble, shout, laugh, pull faces, frighten, enrage, and talk perhaps), in his drawing the head is the chief part, lording it over all the body's parts.

In the beginning, then, the age of the head – a surprising and prophetic insight! Correct from the point of view of the embryologist too: as in all the embryos of mammals the head of the human embryo is unbelievably big...

For the child only the head is indispensable.

A head encounters a head, whereas the feet – a mere appendage – may be missing, likewise the knees and the neck and everything else that will come later. They do not detain him now. This is not yet the age of going back over things.

When he draws he is not copying man; he is making him. Resemblance occurs, crude enough no doubt. A similarity, and the child is beside himself with delight, he has begun something, and although what he has discovered so far is only a morsel, it is the most essential and in many of the mind's operations it will return.
A first welcome. Simplicity.

A shapeless, misshapen body, still lacking arms, or the arms not properly attached, come out of the neck, or from anywhere,

poitrine, bâtons, balais de bout en bout traversant l'enveloppe du buste, bras pour s'étendre, se détendre, pour s'étirer.

Mais au loin, plus loin encore, le plus loin possible, doigts étendus raides, doigts de l'extrême de soi.

Plaisirs qu'il découvre.

Surface sans masse, un simple fil entoure le vide de l'être, le corps sans corps.

Homme-sac, c'est tout, c'est assez, par deux trous dans le haut regardant. Homme à la grosse tête.

Un sac, n'est-ce pas étrange? Mais ne vivait-il pas déjà – avant de venir respirer au-dehors – et pendant des mois, enveloppé?

Souvent, invité à dessiner un bonhomme, il oublie les jambes, les bras, et que son anatomie est faite pour le déplacement. On dirait que la mobilité, il n'a pas encore opté pour: au moins elle n'est pas ressentie comme essentielle.

Grand, c'est un père; moins grand, avec des paquets, une mère, femme d'avant la sensualité des contours, avec l'arrondi équivoque des seins.

Debout, un poteau à deux jambes; donc un homme; près d'un autre qui n'en a qu'une et ronde tout à fait: donc un arbre.

Comme les arbres sont proches des hommes! Les hommes, presque des arbres, à peu de chose près comme tout est homme!

Maison aux fenêtres observatrices, grande figure par laquelle on va par un sentier dans la campagne.

Chemin au-devant pour accueillir, tel un souhait de bienvenue, chemin afin de tranquilliser, de rassurer dès le départ et la porte toujours bien notée, la porte... à ne pas manquer, par où s'introduire en la protection de la demeure... et la poignée que souvent il dessine dès le début, l'utile et difficile poignée.

Les plus imprécises approximations ne gênent pas l'enfant. Ce qui compte c'est le *rapprochement*. Ce rapprochement, trouvé et retrouvé, vient ouvrir de façon claire une porte qui en ouvrira quantité d'autres. Large porte de la connivence.

Que l'homme dessiné par lui, paraisse aux yeux d'adultes plutôt une perche, un têtard géant, un clown, un gros boudin ou une énorme betterave importe peu. Par une ligne la transmission s'est operée.

out of the head or the chest, sticks, broomhandles end to end across the upper body, arms to spread out with, to relax with, to stretch.

But further away, further still, at the furthest possible, fingers stretched out stiffly, fingers at the limits of the self.

Pleasures he is discovering.

A surface without mass, a simple thread surrounds the emptiness of the creature, a body without body.

A sack-man, that is all, that is enough, through two holes in the upper part looking out. The man with the big head.

A sack, is that not strange? But has he not already lived – before coming out to breathe – and lived for months, enclosed?

Often if he is asked to draw a little man he forgets the arms and legs and that his anatomy equips him to be mobile. It is as though he has not yet opted for mobility: at least, mobility is not felt to be essential.

A large figure is a father; less large, with bundles, a mother, a woman by the sensuality of her outline, with the ambiguous roundness of her breasts.

Upright, a post with two legs; a man therefore; next to another with only one and quite round: a tree.

How close trees are to men! Men very nearly trees, and how like everything nearly is to men!

A house with windows watching you, a big face from which by a path you go into the country.

A path at the front to receive you, like the wish for welcome, a path that calms, reassuring at the outset and the door always carefully remembered, the door... that must not be missed, through which to enter into the safeness of the dwelling... and the doorhandle which often he draws first of all, the useful and difficult doorhandle.

The child's approximations may be very rough indeed, but that does not bother him. What matters is: to draw near. In so doing, again and again, he decisively opens a door, which will open more doors, a great number. A wide way in to complicity.

That the man he draws looks, to an adult, more like a post, a giant tadpole, a clown, a big black-pudding or an enormous beetroot matters very little. By means of a line an act of transmission has taken place.

Un corps d'homme vient à lui, un corps ballon, un corps bâton, un corps infirme mais qui suffisamment à son idée fait corps d'homme et, beaucoup mieux, l'être «homme» et, plus étonnant encore, parfois le fait *lui*-même. Son propre être, il retrouve, il l'y voit. En cette enveloppe si frêle, il se met, s'y remet. Il se sent pareil, s'y comparant sans difficulté: un vague dedans qu'une ligne décidée, quoique variable selon l'humeur, sépare du dehors.

L'homme dorénavant retrouvable à volonté. Dans les lignes qui ont cessé d'être explosives, le prodige qui le fait homme, Démarrage-homme.

...tandis que les jeunes chimpanzés ou gorilles, faiseurs de cercles approximatifs, qui égalaient souvent ceux des enfants, en restent au même point, au même plaisir.

Si nombreuses que soient les lignes incurvées qu'ils font, jamais aucun d'eux n'y reconnaît ni un corps ni la forme de qui ou de quoi que ce soit et ne s'y arrête.

Peut-être faudrait-il les mettre d'une certaine façon sur le chemin.

Dessiner, c'est représenter, présenter à nouveau, donc imiter. Curieux que le singe si imitateur, là n'imite pas.

L'enfant, lui, dès les premiers jours de sa découverte, se retrouve, a affaire aux êtres et aux choses sans avoir à les chercher dans ses lignes. Il ne revient plus en arrière.

Il a vu la correspondance, que le singe ne voit pas, il l'a saisie, la ressuscite, réalisant en cela plus pleinement la condition humaine que son ancêtre venant de trouver la roue ou bien le feu à partir du frottement de bois taillés.

Rapprochements, relation enclenchante qui ne disparaît plus, qui devient une habitude vitale et en constante extension.

Corps de pères, corps de mères, corps de petits, de tout-petits et de chats et de chiens.

Quant aux arbres à trois ou quatre branches ou bras, il suffira d'autant de traits pour les retrouver entiers... suffisamment.

Sans règles encore, sans compromis, sans appliquer de lois, dessin qui est allusion plutôt que description.

...et jeu.

Parfois un enfant au visage grave dessine, au scandale de l'entourage, un père hurluberlu et joue sans respect avec lui, manipulant le personnage selon son plaisir, selon ses surprises, ses ravissements...

Jeu que gestes encore peu adroits suscitent ou augmentent, une

A man's body comes to him, a balloon body, a stick body, a body which though rather shaky is near enough his idea of the body of a man and, even better, of the creature "man", and at times, even more surprisingly, his idea of the fact of *himself.* He finds his own being there, he sees it. Again and again he envelops himself, easily compares himself to it: a vague interior separated from outside by a line that is decisive but may vary according to mood.

Man henceforth able to be found again at will. In lines that have ceased to be explosive the miracle that makes him a man, Man-who-sets-out.

... whereas young chimpanzees or gorillas, though they draw rough circles too and often no worse than those that children draw, they never get beyond that stage, beyond that pleasure.

However many curving lines they do not one of them ever sees a body there or the shape of anyone or anything at all and halts at it.

Perhaps we should find a way of starting them off.

To draw is to represent, to present again, which is: to imitate. Curious that the monkey, so good at imitation, never imitates when he draws.

But the child, once he has made his discovery, discovers himself in it, and deals with creatures and with things whose presence in his drawings is obvious to him.. He never regresses.

He has seen the correspondence that the monkey does not see, he has grasped it, he revives it, and realises the human condition more fully by doing so than his ancestors did in inventing the wheel or in making fire by rubbing two sticks together.

Acts of bringing close, of bringing into relationship... This ability will always be there now. It will become a vital habit, constantly being extended.

Bodies of fathers, bodies of mothers, bodies of babies, of tiny babies and of cats and dogs.

As for the trees with three or four branches or arms, that number of lines is enough and the trees are complete... complete enough.

Still without rules, without compromises, without recourse to laws – that sort of drawing is more allusion than description.

... and play.

Sometimes a child, with a serious look, will shock the company by drawing an outlandish father and playing games with him. Has he no respect? He manhandles the figure to please, surprise and delight himself...

It is a game which the still unskilful movements of his hand start

menotte sans assurance le suscite et l'entretient.

Se plaisant à être tantôt plus près, tantôt plus loin du modèle, ne cherchant pas à l'égaler, jouant (entre autres) à être le père et pas lui et tout de même lui, en approximations dérisoires qui le divertissent.

Jeu naturel, sinon innocent du moins plaisant mais sans insister, père en passant, père négligemment. Un père bien relâché, à la tête mal venue... grand, allongé plutôt, interminable.

La maison se présente et se représente à lui. Quelques traits d'un seul élan sans fléchir font des lignes droites et les droites font naturellement des maisons assez approchantes, avec porte, fenêtres, et toit. Ce n'est pas difficile. On y ajoute le chemin, sinueux de préférence, amusant à faire, si nécessaire, si parlant, comme trajet, et aussi comme élément premier d'orientation – précaution à ne pas oublier.

L'enfant en ses dessins évoque la maison, la *pense* pour y aller, pour y retourner quand il le faudra, répète son plaisir d'y revenir, établit ses repères.

B

Lorsque à l'enfant on fournit (souvent trop tôt) crayons et pots de couleurs, alors après quelques essais, sur sa feuille vierge se répand comme une inondation, une fête inconnue, porteuse de beaucoup d'autres. L'investigateur et schématique dessin qu'il pratiquait rétrocède.

Couleur à présent et sa splendeur. Tout va en recevoir de l'ampleur.

Étalement, étalement, épanchements, remplissages. Envahissement des surfaces, épaississements des formes. Tissu, matière.

La précédente percée par le graphisme, qui allait à signaler, situer, indiquer, fait place aux ENCHANTEMENTS.

Ses dessins d'ailleurs, fût-ce du père, de la mère, ou des frères, n'avaient jamais été des images, mais une idée qui lui venait, un

off and develop, a child's uncertain hand starts it off, keeps it going.

He likes coming close to the model, he likes moving away again, he is not trying to be the same as it, he is playing at being (among other things) the father, but not him, and yet him, in laughable approximations by which he is amused.

These games come naturally and are, if not innocent, amusing at least, and never too serious: he is a father in passing, a father carelessly. A very casual father, with a botched sort of head... large, rather elongated, unending.

The house presents itself and re-presents itself to him. A few strokes at one go, boldly, make the straight lines, and straight lines naturally make a house, one that looks quite like, with a door, windows and roof. It isn't hard. Then the path, preferably winding, fun to do, and so necessary, so expressive, as a little journey and also as a first principle of orientation – a precaution, not to be forgotten.

The child in his drawings evokes the house, *thinks* it, to go in, to come home to when necessary, he repeats the pleasure of homecoming, establishes his landmarks.

B

When (often too soon) a child is given coloured crayons and paints, on to the virgin paper then, after one or two tries, there comes, like a flood, an unprecedented carnival in which many other carnivals are borne along. The drawing he has done so far, exploratory and schematic in its nature, is now superseded.

For the present: colour, and its splendour. Everything now will receive fullness from colour.

A spreading, a spread, outpourings, a giving to things their fill. The invasion of surfaces, the deepening of shapes. Texture, matter.

The first breakthrough, by drawing, which served to make signs, to situate, to point out, gives way now to ACTS OF MAGIC.

The drawings he did before, of father, mother, brothers were never pictures but an idea which came to him, a diagram that sug-

schéma qui se proposait à lui, à son esprit en songeant à eux, vite réalisé en tracés rapides, comme il convient à une attention de brève durée, pour une reconnaissance-éclair.

Cela ne vient plus. Il est débordé par les couleurs qui seront étalées comme des tapis.

Parfois, fonçant, il applique en sauvage ce commode couvre-tout éclatant. Et apparaît un «Carnaval», une foire vers quoi il tendait.

Un œil jeune aime recevoir la sensation à son sommet. Semblablement, on aspire aussi à percevoir le plus de cris perçants possible pour les délices de son ouïe toute fraîche, laquelle au contraire de celle des plus âgés n'en est pas éprouvée.

Qui pourrait à l'égal de l'enfant ressentir l'impact de la couleur rouge?

Tel jeune sanguin à l'appel de son grand appétit de vie, va en étendre de larges bancs pour sa joie incomparable, pour sa stimulation. Atout rouge. Il ne va pas se priver d'un pareil médium de vie et de violence.

Tel autre ce sera le vert (ou l'orange ou le bleu) son unique véhicule, couleur par laquelle tout devra passer et qui le fixe étrangement. *Son* vert. Pendant des jours, des semaines parfois, il n' accepte pas de la mêler à d'autres.

Plus généralement quand l'enfant s'empare des couleurs, c'est leur polyvalence tapageuse, leur tohubohu qui l'excitent, où il passe et repasse comme au milieu de détonations. Un barbouillage peut s'ensuivre qui ne le fait pas reculer, à quoi il n'est pas opposé.

Enfants des villes, privés de la nature et en Occident privés de mythes, ils vont en des ateliers construits pour eux, trouver permis ce qui leur est interdit ailleurs. Là, fasciné par la boue, la vase, les consistances molles, les coulées et ses matières mêmes sorties puantes de ses intestins, le gamin resté intrigué par l'état d'avant la séparation du liquide et du solide, de la terre et de l'eau, d'avant la mise à part du sale et du propre (cette propreté et netteté impeccable qui est le contentement et l'aspiration quasi maniaque de l'adulte) va enfin pouvoir modeler, pétrir le sale, le salissant, et par couches épaisses répandre des coulées de couleurs, sans retenue avec une joie sans nom qui le libère mais gêne les grandes personnes qui le voient faire, barbouillé et heureux.

gested itself, that came to mind when he thought of them, and he set it down quickly, with rapid lines, as is proper when the attention is only briefly held, when the insight comes like lightning.

That no longer happens. He is overwhelmed by colours, he will lay them out like carpets.

Sometimes he lays on colour in a violent haste, like a savage. What else obliterates so brilliantly? And a "carnival" appears, the fair he was making for.

The eyes of a child love to perceive things at their most intense. Likewise his hearing: shouts delight his unaccustomed ears, as loud and as many as possible, such as would be a torment to a grown-up.

Who can feel as intensely as a child the impact of the colour red?

One child in his passion, in his lust for life, will spread great layers of red across the page, it delights him beyond words, it excites him. Red is trumps. He will never relinquish it, like nothing else it is a means of life and violence.

For another the unique medium will be green (or orange or blue), that will be the colour through which everything has to pass and which compels him strangely. *His* green. For days, sometimes for weeks, he will refuse to mix it with any other colours.

More often when a child seizes hold of colours it is their rowdy polyvalence, their hubbub, that excites him, he goes to and fro among them as if among explosions. A mess may ensue, but it does not repel him, he has no objection to messes.

Children who live in towns and are deprived of nature and, in the west, deprived of myths, being let into studios made just for them are allowed to do things there which are forbidden them elsewhere. Fascinated by mud, by slime, by soft consistencies, by things that flow and even by the substances that come out stinking from his own intestines; intrigued by the state before the separation of liquids and solids, of earth and water, and before the setting apart of dirty and clean (the perfect cleanliness and tidiness beloved of adults and aspired to by them more or less maniacally); in his studio at last, where things are dirty and where they make him dirty, the child kneads and moulds and lays on colour in thick liquid layers and does so without inhibition and with a nameless joy which sets him free but embarrasses the grown-ups watching him smirched and happy.

Sa naturelle imprudence le pousse en avant. Lui qui ne sait pas encore vraiment marcher, court. Il tombe, se relève et à nouveau court.

Ainsi d'un élan, ne doutant de rien, il entreprend des sujets que tout peintre éviterait. Sans hésiter, il peindra le soleil, le soleil ni plus ni moins, le grand éblouissant soleil...

Départ en aventurier.

Il peint l'étonnant, lui, et pas de sang-froid. Avec son étonnement non disparu, qu'il revit, il représente le baroque, la girafe, le zèbre; l'exultant avion (au moment du décollage) et la locomotive; petit pour qui rien n'est trop grand, ni trop difficile, il rend l'éléphant, l'incroyable, l'extraordinaire éléphant qui n'y perd pas son «extraordinaire».

Il le ferait plutôt plus extraordinaire, étant ouvert et préparé à l'extraordinaire comme au féerique, au merveilleux, au prodigieux. Il leur est accueillant. Il est porté à y croire ainsi qu'au miraculeux. Le plus médiocre entourage, il le voit et le rend étonnant.

Des études ont montré bien des choses cachées sous l'innocence des enfants. Des passions et de l'inavouable passent en eux, qu'on retrouve en les cherchant dans leurs dessins, restés pourtant enfantins et bonhommes.

De tout temps cette bonhomie a frappé, qui réapparaît même dans les périodes graves, qui désarçonne, déclenchant une décontraction amusée chez les soucieux adultes.

Combien différents de leurs visages tendus et résolus, ceux qu'évoque l'enfant en ses dessins.

Vides, non préoccupés, non déterminés, confiants, ébahis, bonasses, qu'on n'a pas à affronter, visages – fenêtres ouvertes.

Faces crédules, indéfendues, lunaires, non combatives, non résolues, pas prêtes à l'attaque ou à la contre-attaque, solaires quelques-unes.

Le tout-petit garde en lui beaucoup d'inoffensif. Pervers, s'il l'est, méchant quand il l'est, il manque de moyens.

Ses dessins sont ceux d'un démuni. Même malsains ou portant la marque du psychotique, un air d'impuissance infantile y reste collé. Méchant s'il va le devenir, il n'en a pas réalisé la constitution. Il lui en reste des virginités à perdre et à percer. Ce dépen-

His natural boldness pushes him on. Though he cannot walk properly yet, he runs. Falls down, gets up and runs again.

Likewise, at a bound, with never a doubt, he takes on subjects any painter would avoid. No hesitations: he will paint the sun, neither more nor less, the big and blinding sun...

He sets off on adventures.

He paints astonishing things, and not cold-bloodedly either. Amazement is in him still, he relives it, he depicts curiosities, the giraffe, the zebra; the exultant aeroplane (at the moment of take-off) and the locomotive; small as he is, nothing is too big for him, nor too difficult, he does the elephant, the unbelievable extraordinary elephant; and the elephant, in being done, loses nothing of its "extraordinariness".

More likely he will make it more extraordinary, since he is open to the extraordinary and prepared for it, just as he is for the magical, the marvellous, the phenomenal. He welcomes them. He is inclined to believe in them, and in miracles. Whatever his surroundings, however unremarkable, when he looks at them he renders them amazing.

Studies have brought to light all sorts of things that were hidden beneath the innocence of children. Passions and things that cannot be admitted come and go in them, and can be discerned, if looked for, in their drawings which remain nevertheless childish and good-humoured.

This good humour has often been remarked upon. Even at serious times it reappears. Adults, always anxious, are nonplussed by it, and shocked into smiling.

How different from their tense and resolute faces are the faces the child evokes in his drawings.

Vacant, not preoccupied, not determined, trusting, flabbergasted, easygoing, no need to confront them – their faces are open windows.

Credulous, undefended faces, moonlike, not belligerent, not resolute, not about to attack or counter-attack, sun-like some of them.

Still there in the child is much that is inoffensive. Perverse he might be, bad sometimes, but he lacks the means.

His drawings are those of somebody unequipped. Even when they are unwholesome or marked by psychosis they still have an air of childish impotence about them. He may turn out bad in the end but as yet he has not realised that potential. He still has virginities to lose

dant ne pourrait l'avoir oublié.

Dès la naissance à la merci des grands qui le pourvoient de tout, mal défendu, il est proche des clowns. Le clown: celui qui reçoit des coups, n'arrive pas à les rendre, voudrait bien, en reçoit davantage, dépourvu de dureté dans un monde dur. Il fascine les enfants qui en rient follement ou pleurent désolés, concernés.

Les personnages figurant dans des peintures d'enfants, comme facilement ils prennent l'air clown, l'air sage aussi et soumis! Jusqu' aux maisons qui ont l'air sage et gentil.

Dans cette période de son existence où tout est reçu, tout aussi est apparenté à celui qui récemment encore ne pouvait s'emparer de rien. À voir (chez les fillettes surtout) des lieux sans doute quelconques, qu'elles ont peints, cours, chambrettes, potagers ou jardinets, on se croirait dans un univers de cadeaux.

Avant de savoir intelligiblement parler, l'enfant en marmottant, en murmurant, conte. Il conte aussi en ses dessins. Récits dont ne reste que de muets personnages sur la feuille blanche.

En d'autres temps, la tête pleine de contes, avide il en redemandait toujours. Le plus turbulent y devenait sage.

Religieusement les petits écoutaient le religieux et le non-religieux à la fois, le merveilleux. Ils s'y équipaient.

Dans nombre de villages du continent africain des enfants noirs connaissaient encore le plaisir d'entendre de la bouche des anciens, calmes et graves, les récits des merveilles toujours frais de l'histoire du monde, le lièvre savant et rusé, les animaux de bon conseil et les périls rencontrés par la lune.

Dans la case les parents participent, y croyant, ou pas loin d'y croire.

Là les dessins d'enfants sont plus conteurs, plus ostensiblement conteurs, et leurs personnages plus en mouvement, plus en action.

Ailleurs encore dans le monde les dessins d'enfants plus qu'on ne pense, racontent, veulent raconter. Là où les aînés reconnaissent aussitôt et revoient les formes du connu, l'enfant poursuit son voyage inconnu dans l'Inconnu.

Porté toujours à l'incroyable, à y croire, à accepter l'extraordinaire (pour lui tellement vraisemblable), allié d'avance à l'impossi-

and to take. Dependent as he is, how could he have forgotten his dependence?

Having been since birth at the mercy of grown-ups who provide him with everything and being only poorly defended, he is close to the clown. The clown: who gets the stick, who never manages to give it back, who would like to, who gets more stick. He lacks hardness in a hard world. He fascinates the children. He makes them laugh, or they break their hearts weeping on his account.

How easily the figures in children's paintings take on a clown-ish air, and also how well-behaved they look and docile. Even the houses look well-behaved and friendly.

At this period of their lives when everything is given them everything is also related to their still recent selves when they were not able to take possession of anything. Especially the places little girls paint, quite ordinary places − backyards, attic rooms, little plots and gardens − it is like being in a world of presents.

Even before he can talk intelligibly the child mutters and mur-murs stories. In his drawings too he tells stories. Stories that leave nothing behind but unspeaking figures on the white page.

In former times, his head full of stories, greedily he asked for more and more. And however noisy then he quietened down.

Religiously children listened to religious and unreligious things alike. They listened to marvels. And in so doing they equipped themselves.

In many African villages black children still had the pleasure of hearing their elders, calm and serious, recount the never-fading wonders of the history of the world: the wise and canny hare, the trusty, helpful animals, and the perils encountered by the moon.

Indoors, their parents take part, believing or nearly believing.

There when the children draw they are more obviously telling stories and their characters move more and do more.

And elsewhere in the world children's drawings, more than one might think, tell stories or try to. Where older people immediately recognise and re-encounter forms of the known, the child goes his unknown way into the unknown.

Forever disposed towards the unbelievable, disposed to believe it, to accept the extraordinary (in his eyes so plausible), already in

ble (aimé autrefois des prophètes qui le donnaient pour modèle), il est, malgré les nouveaux obstacles, ouvert comme il ne le sera jamais plus; près des miracles, des miracles en tout genre pour lesquels il désirerait des explications sans barrière, ces réponses miracles qui n'abaissent pas, mais emplissent l'être d'émotions exaltantes.

... Celui qui ne sait pas ou si peu et si mal sait aussi quelque chose. Sans pouvoir, il tient un autre pouvoir. Les petits apportent à la peinture des espaces libérés de l'Espace. Ils sont des centaines qui tout seuls, en d'autres temps aussi bien que dans celui-ci, ont fait mieux que de retrouver l'espace babylonien avec le dessin dit «à rabattement», raccourci devenu là-bas un procédé. Ils ont trouvé, quand ils en avaient besoin et selon leur envie, la *simultanéité*, celle qui unit et combine le vu et le connu, le vu par l'œil et le connu par l'esprit, le lointain avec le proche, le dedans avec le dehors lequel cesse de le dissimuler.

Tout naturellement un enfant mettra ensemble la façade avec le mur du fond qu'il ne pourrait apercevoir, mais qu'il *sait là*. Et pareillement pour son plaisir un mur de la maison se troue et se dissipe afin qu'apparaisse le désirable intérieur où il va se rendre pour manger à la table déjà mise.

Spontanément, non comme une recette d'atelier, les enfants, traducteurs d'espaces, montrent ce qu'avec bonheur on retrouve, la *coexistence du vu et du conçu*, qui a lieu en tout cerveau qui évoque. On commence par là. C'est l'enfant et non l'homme fait, qui ici est fidèle à la réalité.

Problème, un des plus difficiles à résoudre, si on ne veut pas simplement l'écarter par des considérations sur la perspective et l'optique et pire, par une restreignante photographie.

Les manques de l'enfant font son génie.

Après des mois sans bouger, sans vue dans une enveloppe de chair, arrivé misérable à l'air libre, sans préparation en un monde nouveau, lui-même nouveau, des membres appliqués sur lui, dont il ne sait que faire, devenu une boule de malaise, de faim, de soif, de manque et d'impéritie, le voici appelé à se mouvoir, à faire que se meuvent muscles et articulations. En pleine aventure pendant longtemps, il se meut avançant à quatre pattes. Comme il est naturel que dans ses dessins il ne mette pas à ce corps, à demi

league with the impossible (beloved of the prophets who held it up as a model), the child, despite the new obstacles, is more open than he will ever be again; he lives among miracles, among miracles of every kind, and would like them explained, quite openly, with miraculous explanations which will not depress his soul but uplift it and fill it full.

... Not knowing or knowing so little and knowing it so badly, still he knows something. Powerless, he has power of another kind. Children bring to their paintings spaces freed from Space. Hundreds of them, all on their own, begin to use space as the Babylonians did; and by a short-cut *they* developed into a technique a child will open his pictures out. He has discovered – when he needed to and as he pleased – *simultaneity*, which unites and combines things seen and things known, things seen by the eye, things known by the mind, near and far, inside and an outside ceasing to conceal it.

A child will quite naturally put together the outside wall with the wall at the back which he cannot see but which he *knows is there*. And similarly, to please him, holes will appear in the wall of a house or it will vanish and the inside will appear, because that is what he wants to see, and in he goes to eat at the table already laid.

Spontaneously, not working to order as a professional might, children, who are translators of space, show us a thing it makes us happy to encounter, the *coexistence of what is seen and what is conceived*, a coming together which takes place whenever the mind imagines. That is how we begin. The child, not the grown man, is true to reality. It is a problem, and one of the hardest to solve. We can always bypass it, of course, by discussing perspective or optics instead, or, worse still, by limiting ourselves to photography.

The child's deficiencies are what constitutes his genius.

After months immobile and sightless under a wrapping of skin he lands in the open air unhappily, in a new world, unprepared, being new himself, with limbs attached that he does not know how to manage, he is nothing but discomfort, hunger, thirst, want and haplessness... Whereupon, in that state, he is required to become mobile and to exercise his muscles and his joints. For a long time his very existence is an adventure, and he moves, he makes progress, on all fours. So it is natural that in his drawings he should put feet

étranger, les pieds et les bras et les mains à leur juste emplacement, ni au même endroit deux fois de suite; accidents de cette «vie à membres» pas encore tout à fait adoptée.

N'y pas voir seulement des signes d'anomalies. Il n'a que quelques douzaines de mois de cette vie d'efforts et de malheureuses manœuvres.

Si ses mouvements restent imparfaits et ses muscles insuffisamment exercés, d'invisibles impulsions le parcourent, désirs de mouvements «autres». Incomparablement plus que l'adulte, l'enfant s' imagine volant, planant, grimpant, galopant ou nageant comme un poisson, rampant comme un reptile. Voilà qui est loin du dessein primordial de l'adulte qui est de *fixer*, et en peinture d'établir des constats visuels.

Par ses multiples identifications, génératrices d'espaces, l'enfant constamment s'y trouve projeté, pareil à un oiseau qui serait aussi un coursier.

Tel est un de ses commencements

...qui aura une fin. L'enfant devient ce qu'il voulait et qu'on voulait pour lui.

Tout mis en place, réglé, situé, stabilisé. Plus de raisons d'avoir des espaces en plus. Il ne les *sent plus*.

C

Avaleur avide dès sa naissance l'enfant devient enfant-bouche. Cela au moins ne le fait pas souffrir, ne le bouscule pas, ne le blesse pas, arrête ses pleurs.

Téter, embrasser le monde et puis dormir.

Tenant le sein, retenant le sein, sans même savoir ce qu'est le sein, sein donné, excellence sans comparaison.

En ses premières années, vivre, c'est *être ouvert*... aux sons, aux couleurs, aux odeurs, aux mouvements, aux gestes; tout à prendre, à apprendre.

Faisant ce qu'il voit faire, le refaisant, copiant, apprenant en imitant, ramassant tout ce qu'il peut.

Après les crayonnages, la découverte et le maniement des couleurs, après leur assimilation et leur pratique, il arrive à plus

and arms and handes on his still unfamiliar body not where they belong and not in the same place twice; in this "life with limbs", which he has still not completely adopted, naturally he makes mistakes.

Not to be thought of as a mere malfunctioning. He will have only a few dozen months of this life of exertion and unhappy manoeuvring.

His movements may remain unaccomplished and his muscles insufficiently exercised, but invisible impulses are coming and going in him: he would like to make "other" movements. Far, far more than any adult the child imagines himself flying, floating, climbing, galloping or swimming like a fish, crawling like a reptile. This is a long way from the adult's primordial aim which is to *fix*, and in painting to establish visual markers.

By his manifold acts of identification, which generate spaces, the child is constantly projected into them, like a bird and a fabulous steed in one.

This, then, is one of his beginnings.

... which will have an end. The child becomes what he wanted and what was wanted for him.

Everything in its place, regulated, situated, stabilised. No more reasons for having extra spaces. He no longer *feels* them.

C

From the day he arrives a child is a greedy swallower. He becomes all mouth. There at least he is not made to suffer, he is not jostled or hurt and his tears are stilled.

To suck, to kiss the world and then to sleep.

Holding the breast, holding on to the breast, without even knowing what it is, the given breast, there is nothing comparable.

In his first years to be alive is *to be open*... to sounds, colours, smells, movements, gestures; all things are there for the taking, for the taking in.

Doing what he sees done, doing it again, copying it, learning by imitating, gathering all he can.

After the drawings, after the discovery and the first handling of colours, after their assimilation and their use, a child may then –

d'un – et toujours avant l'adolescence – de réaliser des peintures chargées. Un je ne sais quoi sur elles retient le regard.

Il ne rend plus un visage ni ne l'évoque, il répand un visage et ce faisant répand un monde. Visage dilaté, béat ou rayonnant, comme il n'en fera plus un pareil plus tard, exprimant sans vergogne son plaisir, y compris celui de sa santé, de sa vitalité débordante, étant à l'âge où on n'a pas honte de montrer son plaisir.

Fini les figures étriquées qui faisaient sourire les adultes à l'air supérieur; maintenant dans la profusion des couleurs presque difficiles à supporter, il s'élargit: visages mêmes de l'ouverture, du rayonnement, sans recul, étalés, impudents. Après ils se refermeront.

Chez la fillette, les fleurs plutôt viennent prendre la place, pas en grand nombre, souvent même une seule, haute sur une tige sans accident, corolle à quatre pétales, et tellement grande ouverte, cette corolle, bien en vue, heureuse de se montrer, qui n'a pas peur, qui a patience.

La fondamentale ouverture n'est pas encore en vue pourtant. Serait-elle pressentie? Fleur telle quelle jour après jour répétée.

Une fleur pour se résumer. Fleur, ça doit suffire.

Mais à l'intérieur de l'enfant comme en son extérieur, un homme ou une femme est à venir, où la famille avec amusement croit reconnaître un parent à quelque trait. D'autres particularités seront passagères. Dans des dessins trop colorés ou trop peu, des reproches, des ressentiments, des appels, des colères, des imaginations ou seulement des empreintes.

Parmi les enfants de toute sorte, ouverts, il en est de moins ouverts et que précisément leurs dessins – ironie du sort – trahiront plus que les autres.

Moins enfantines que leur voix, leurs destinées.

Tel ou tel, loin déjà, est devenu inintéressable. Les lignes, les couleurs, il ne va plus se fourrer là-dedans. Il reste là où lui s'est mis, où l'on ne le piégera pas. Il n'est pas de montagnes, aux pics aigus comme des epées, ni de corps maltraités, morcelés, ensanglantés qui pourraient l'exprimer.

Au-delà de l'agressivité, au-delà de la colère, il entre dans le mauvais vouloir intégral.

always before adolescence – begin to paint pictures that are laden. Something about them fascinates.

Now he neither depicts nor evokes a face, he puts them forth and in doing so it is a whole world he puts forth. Wide open faces, blissful or beaming, faces such as later he will never do again, quite shamelessly they demonstrate his pleasure, including the pleasure his healthiness gives him, his superabundance of vitality, for he is young enough not to be ashamed of showing pleasure.

No more of those crabbed little figures that made the grown-ups smile their superior smiles; now in all the almost overwhelming abundance of colour he is enlarged: these are the very faces of opening up, of beaming, they are displayed, they have no shame, in them there is no going back. Later they will close up again.

For little girls it is not so much faces as flowers, and not in any great number, often only one, high up on a bare stalk, four-petalled, and so very wide open, in full view, happy to show itself, fearless and patient.

The deepest opening is not yet in sight however. Anticipated perhaps? Repeating an ordinary flower day after day.

A flower to say all that is necessary about herself.

But inside the child, as in its outward appearance too, a man or a woman is coming into being, in whom the family are amused to discover (as they believe) the traits of a parent or a relative. Other characteristics do not last. They are there in the too richly or too sparsely coloured pictures: grievance, resentment, need, anger, fantasy – traces at least.

Among the many kinds of children, all open, there are some who are less open, and they are the ones – ironically – whose drawings will most give them away.

Their destinies are less childish than their voices.

This one or that, already distant, has ceased to be able to be interested. He will no longer engross himself in lines and colours. He stays where by his own design he has put himself – where no one will trap him. Neither mountains with peaks as sharp as swords nor even maltreated bodies, however hacked and bloody, will suffice as images of his state.

He is beyond aggressiveness, beyond anger, he is entering into

Bouderie d'enfant, arme pour qui en a si peu, et que plus d'un gamin, que plus d'une gamine découvre un jour ou l'autre, contre laquelle il n'y aura pas une parade facile.

Refus. *Non* à la participation, au manger, au parler, à la marche, aux jeux mêmes.

Plus fortement qu'on ne croit, l'enfant connaît la tentation de s'arrêter, de ne plus se laisser entraîner sur la voie du développement où on le mène, aux efforts qui n'en finissent pas, à l'apprentissage toujours plus compliqué... Est-ce qu'il continue? ou va-t-il s'arrêter?

Il y a seulement quelques dizaines de mois il était dans le non-événement. Pas de problèmes, pas de recherches, pas d'efforts; pour se nourrir, pas avoir à mettre en mouvement les muscles masticatoires. À présent, incessante coordination de mouvements à apprendre, pour monter, descendre, sauter, se retourner, pour ceci pour cela, pour enjamber, toujours à recommencer, à perfectionner.

Avant, sans rien faire, il aboutissait toujours à l'île maternelle, à la source, à l'universel.

Dégoût. Répulsion. Quelque obscure déficience du corps le gêne, le retient. Il a des empêchements. Il en rajoute. Il prend leur parti. Refus. Résistances. Mutisme.

La tentation qui ramène l'enfant en arrière ne peut se comparer à une révolte. Plus interne. Plus absolue. Dans quelque temps on n'obtiendra plus de lui aucune participation.

Grève, la plus primitive. Une aventure aussi, monde irrévélé aux autres.

Sans parler, il a dit adieu aux adultes et aux garçons et filles de son âge, qui se sont soumis.

Il n'a plus de compagnons, partis ceux-ci pour l'enrégimentement «adulte».

Retour au commencement, refuge qui devient impasse. Ascèse également, on peut l'appeler ainsi, ascèse malheureuse d'un petit et combien dure! Elle le tient maintenant enfermé.

Quel dommage qu'on ne puisse voir dans son esprit comme on pouvait voir dans les dessins.

total malevolence.

Sulking is one of the few weapons children have. There comes a time when boys and girls discover it, and countering it will be hard.

Refusal. *No* to joining in, to eating, speaking, walking or even playing.

The child, far more than we care to believe, is tempted to call a halt, to refuse to be dragged any further along the way of development, tempted to resist the neverending efforts, the ever more complicated apprenticeship... Will he go on? or will he stop?

Only a few dozen months ago his world was the world of non-event. No problems, no need to go looking or exert himself; to feed, it was not even necessary to work his jaws. And now he must learn and forever practise the coordination of his movements, to climb up or down, to jump, turn around, for this or that, to get astride, and always to be begun again, to be got right.

Before, without doing anything, it was always the maternal island he came to at last, to the source, to a universal place.

Disgust. Repulsion. Some obscure deficiency in his body troubles him, holds him back. Things hamper him. He adds to them. He sides with them. Refusal. Acts of resistance. Speechlessness.

The temptation which pulls a child back cannot be compared to a revolt. More inward. More absolute. Before long he will refuse all cooperation.

A strike, the most primitive. An adventure too, a world not revealed to others.

Without a word he has said goodbye to the adults and to the boys and girls of his own age who have submitted.

All his companions have left him – for the regimented "adult" world.

Back to the beginning, retreat into an impasse. Or it might equally well be called a discipline, a child's ascetic discipline, unhappy and how hard.

What a pity we cannot see into his soul as we could into the drawings.

Toutefois, l'activité cérébrale ne pouvant en sa totalité être immobilisée, il arrive qu'un arriéré, s'étant adonné en secret à une suractivité locale, se montre un jour, à l'étonnement général, calculateur hors de l'ordinaire, capable à une vitesse déconcertante de calculer mentalement, à la demande, tel ou tel nombre énorme d'heures écoulées depuis une certaine date du Moyen Âge ou de l'Égypte ptolémaïque. Et toute autre vaine prouesse arithmétique il réussit.

Sous l'apathie générale s'était cachée une mobilisation ponctuelle, maintenue et développée en silence, l'aidant à passer sa longue nuit.

Savoir-faire isolé, insuffisant mais lorsque les autres s'en aperçoivent, un étendard quand même, son étendard là, relevé.

And yet, since mental activity cannot be halted entirely, it may happen that a backward child, having been in secret hyperactive in one particular zone, one day reveals himself, amid general astonishment, to be extraordinarily good at mental arithmetic: he can work out, on demand, at frightening speed, what vast number of hours have elapsed since a certain date in the Middle Ages or Ancient Egypt. And any other such useless feats of arithmetic, he can always manage them.

Beneath a general apathy there lay hidden this ability to mobilise rapidly and exactly his mental powers – an ability nurtured and developed in silence and that helps him get through the long night he is in.

A solitary power, insufficient but, when others notice it, a banner nevertheless, his own, uplifted.

Par surprise

By surprise

...après ce que j'ai sans raison avalé, qui présentement me monte à la tête – déjà plus tout à fait «ma» tête – et qui va incessamment l'amener, vacillante, à me tromper, à errer, je le sais, je le sens, à m'aliéner...

...absorbée sans prendre garde, tout en songeant à autre chose, à un départ, à un voyage, la plaquette brune, retrouvée dans le fond d'un tiroir avec de vieilles bricoles, cadeau d'une fille de bonne volonté...

...cela que tout de suite mais trop tard je repousse, qui de son côté me repousse, creuse en moi ses chemins sans s'occuper des miens, et m'écarte si vite, que je ne sais comment agir, m'attaque et n'est personne, n'a pas besoin d'être une personne et à grandes baffes brutalement sur ma zone à réfléchir, frappe et bouscule.

...le domicile de ma tête, sans que j'y puisse rien maintenant, je vais le perdant... JE VAIS LE PERDRE.

Dans mon atelier, passant devant la vue d'un paysage de l'Inde où sont assis deux, trois groupes de campagnardes en sari, à l'ombre d'un banian...

Sous mon regard qui ne s'attendait à rien de tel, paysans et paysannes se meuvent, se remettent à bouger, à l'instant remis de leur immobilisation forcée, retrouvent leurs gestes, reprennent leur marche, mais pas pour aller loin, c'est curieux, seulement pour revenir prendre leur départ une fois, deux fois, plusieurs fois; ainsi font-ils tous et une mule s'ébroue, s'apprêtant au portage, prête à nouveau, prête à nouveau, prête à nouveau.

Des figures, jusque-là simples dessins épinglés au mur, se réveillent, se raniment; leurs traits «fixés» cessent de l'être. Les yeux pleins de vie brillent, les regards ranimés traversent la pièce, semblent vraiment apercevoir ce, ou celui, qu'avec attention ils regardent, sans s'occuper de moi, l'intrus.

Je ne comprends plus, quoiqu'ils voient grâce à «ma» vue singulière, c'est inouï comme ils se passent de moi, ces naïfs, nou-

...after what I have swallowed for no reason and that now is going to my head – already no longer wholly *my* head – and that, I know it, I feel it, will soon induce this unsteady head to lead me astray and get things wrong and deprive me of myself...

...taken inattentively, my mind on something else, departure, journeying, the small brown tablet a willing girl once gave me and I came across at the bottom of a drawer among old odds and ends...

...pushed aside at once but already too late and now, for its part, it pushes me aside and makes its own tracks through me disregarding mine, and removes me so swiftly I am at a loss and attacks me and is nobody and has no need to be anyone and thwacks me brutally where my thinking is and knocks me about.

...the home I had in my head, I am in the process of losing it and cannot help myself... I AM CERTAINLY LOSING IT.

In my studio, passing the picture of a landscape in India in which two or three groups of peasant women wearing saris are sitting in the shade of a banyan tree...

And as I look, expecting nothing of the sort, the peasants, men and women, suddenly recovered from their enforced immobility, stir and begin to move again, they move their hands, they begin to walk again, though not to go very far, how strange, but only to return and set off again, once, twice, several times, all of them do, and a mule gives a shudder, getting ready for carrying things, over and over again.

Faces, until then merely drawings: pinned to the wall, awake and come to life; their "fixed" features cease to be so. The shining eyes are full of life, brightly they look across the room and seem really to see what or whoever they fix on intently, and me, the intruder, they ignore.

I no longer understand: it is thanks to "my" special vision that they can see, but how astonishingly unnecessary I am to them,

131

veaux occupants de mon atelier, où un jour je traçai leurs traits sans même savoir exactement ce que je faisais.

Eux maintenant de leur propre initiative se continuent à part et en force.

Regards, passages, trajectoires (que je sens venir de plusieurs côtés) encombrent la pièce où il n'y a pas de place pour tant de gens, et si intensément observateurs.

Ignorant, inconscient pour avoir avalé cette drogue, en somme quasi pour m'en débarrasser, *j'ai mis en route la roue du temps.*

Les images ne m'intéressent pas, je n'en veux plus. Avec un produit de cette force, ça ne doit pas convenir. Je retourne dans ma chambre afin de me recueillir. Trop tard déjà.

Trouble. Ballottements, déplacements d'un étrange déplacement en diverses zones. L'environnement devient malsain. L'esprit, le mécanisme cérébral achoppe, manœuvrant difficilement. Déplacements pas tout le temps également. Tension, par bouffées douloureuses...

Le concret n'aura pas duré longtemps. Restent les réflexions qui continuent à venir; mais dans quel état! en fragments injustifiés. Des mots renforcés sans raison, soudain frappants, qu'on croit entendre ou dont on éprouve la présence, l'excessive poussée, déséquilibrent la pensée, rendant toute phrase incongrue.

Il faut avoir connu du dedans cette allure particulière, pour savoir comme elle est désarçonnante. Dérèglement qui a dû faire prendre pour atteints de confusion (laquelle n'est que secondaire), certains qui ne l'étaient pas tellement, luttant contre l'apparent charabia pour tenir le cap, le cap malgré tout.

Une soif insensée dans la gorge sèche s'est installée.

...et si je fermais les yeux? Non. Je ne m'y risque pas. Pas prêt à des visions. D'ailleurs le produit – sûrement un mélange – me traite et me maltraite sans images.

Coups, rafales, charges et biais soudains dans les passages pensants, dans les énonciations intérieures, de plus en plus fortes. Pensées décalées, déviées, repoussées, dont je ne peux maintenir la

these innocents, the new occupants of my studio, where one day I sketched them without even properly realising what I was doing.

And now they continue a vigorous existence of their own, apart from me.

Looks, their trajectories, a crisscrossing of glances (which I feel coming at me from all sides) crowd the room which is too small for so many and such intense observers.

In ignorance and unawareness having swallowed the drug – more or less only to get rid of it – *I have set the wheel of time in motion.*

The pictures do not interest me, I have seen enough of them. And doubtless with such a powerful substance looking at pictures is not the thing to do. I go back to my bedroom, to be quiet. Already too late.

Disturbance. Upheaval, displacements of a strange displacement in different zones. The world about me is becoming unhealthy. The mind, the cerebral mechanism, trips, manoeuvres with difficulty. Displacements not always equally. Tension, in waves of pain...

These physical things cannot have lasted long. Thoughts remain, and they keep coming, but what a state they are in! Units that make no sense. Words unreasonably emphasised, suddenly striking words that one seems to hear or whose presence one feels, their untoward impetus throws my thinking off balance and renders every phrase incongruous.

Nobody who has not experienced it from the inside can have any idea how disconcerting this particular condition is. Sometimes such dislocation will occasion a state which may be mistaken for confusion, but is not confusion in any real degree or is it only secondarily; and in that state the mind then struggles against an *apparent* chaos, to hold, come what may, to its own sense of direction.

A ferocious thirst has settled in my dry throat.

...and supposing I closed my eyes? No. I don't dare. I am not ready for visions. Moreover the substance – which I am sure was impure – is continuing to use and abuse me without any images.

Blows, sudden gusts, assaults and lurches in the passages of thought, in the stronger and stronger utterances within me. Thoughts

direction. Idem dans la conduite, idem dans le geste, idem dans les mouvements, eux aussi, même les plus «pratiques», devenant, et pour les mêmes raisons, gauches, hésitants, inutilisables.

Phrases intérieures disloquées. Maintenant toute recherche mentale passe et part sans s'accomplir.

Y revenir? Mais je ne fais que cela.

À la place de l'unité de la phrase, le morcellement, un général morcellement, la prévalence du morcellement, toute situation évolue vers plus de morcellement. J'ai changé de monde pour celui-là qui, serait-il méprisé, *commande*.

Regards sur les infirmités nouveau-nées.

Un simple numéro de téléphone ordinaire, je n'arrive pas à bout de le trouver, de le copier, de le retenir. Je voudrais pourtant tellement entendre les mots banals d'un homme normal à un instant quelconque et une voix simple, tranquille, tranquillisante, loin du tragique. Difficile. À commencer par les chiffres du numéro visé, ils ne peuvent être convenablement alignés. Serait-ce impossible? Dans la phrase qu'ensuite j'aurais à composer, à prononcer et que j'essaie mentalement, déjà je m'embarrasse. Que serait-ce dans la réalité? Me prenant pour un fou, on appellerait au secours un médecin ou la police.

Des coups, des flux, des renversements me débarquent. Je suis, comme entre deux douanes, pris, repris, rejeté. Questions partout. Une constellation d'interrogations qui m'interpelle, me presse, cependant qu'une multiple incertitude s'approfondit.

Bouffonne, pouffante, plus du tout assise la situation. Et quelle impréparation! Je n'en reviens pas, furieusement mécontent contre moi, et honteux.

Tout ca simplifié s'appellerait aussi vertige.

Équilibre, premiers apprentissages du nouveau-né, je les reperds avec en plus quantité de nouveaux, acquis au cours des âges, certains parmi les plus subtils.

Coups de boutoir. Bousculé de plus en plus. Mouvements des mains, des bras, du buste, dès que je change de position, si difficiles à coordonner, et davantage encore ceux des pieds lorsque je me lève.

J'ai seulement de l'équilibre intermittent, que des vagues invisi-

out of time, out of line, pushed aside, and their direction is not in my control. Likewise my behaviour, likewise my gestures, and even my movements, even the most "functional" of them, are becoming, and for the same reason, clumsy, hesitant and useless.

The sentences in my head are all in bits. Now every mental foray lapses without conclusion.

Should I start again? I do nothing else.

Instead of the unity of the sentence there is a breaking down, there is a general breaking down, a predominance of breaking down, every situation evolves towards yet more breaking down. I have changed worlds at the behest of one who, despised though he may be, *is giving the orders.*

I note my newest infirmities.

To find, copy out and remember a simple ordinary telephone number is beyond me. And yet I should so much like to hear the everyday words of a normal man at a given moment, and a simple calm and calming voice, not in the least bit tragic. Difficult. For a start, I cannot get properly into line the figures of the number I have in mind to ring. Perhaps it is impossible. And with the sentence I should then have to compose and utter, even as I rehearse it mentally, already I am in difficulties. What would actually happen? They would think me insane and call a doctor or the police.

Headlong under blows bowled over I am deposited on the shore. I am caught as though between two frontiers and caught again and expelled. Questioning everywhere. Interrogations in a battery come at me, press upon me, and meanwhile a manifold uncertainty only deepens.

My state is comical, farcical and by now very unstable. And such a lack of foresight! It amazes me. I am furious with myself, and ashamed.

More simply you might also call it vertigo.

I am losing my balance and the skills a newborn baby acquires first and others also that come with age and among them the most difficult.

A battering. And ever more violently pushed around. The movements of my hands, my arms, my chest, as soon as I change position are so difficult to co-ordinate and even more so those of my feet when I get up.

I have my balance only intermittently, and when the invisible

bles renversent.

Atteintes aux équilibres. Combien il peut y en avoir. Combien d'inattendus.

Dislocations. Les prises mentales sans force. Je ne m'y attendais pas, pas à celles-là. C'est nouveau.

Je m'étends. Inutile. Le divan, comme s'il n'était plus divan, ..., plus une seconde ne repose. Autant se coucher sur une pelle, sur un râteau. Profitons au moins de cet état. Je peux mieux observer les procédés du cerveau, le mode suivant lequel il continue point par point à raisonner, comme si de rien n'était, pianotant sur les données encore en sa possession. Ah! la logique, l'imperturbée logique avec ses montages qui ne peuvent aboutir, et qu'elle continue bravement à faire, accumulant immanquablement erreur sur erreur! Quel spectacle!

Je suis loin de saisir et d'apprécier ce qui exactement est bousculé en moi, et qui me trouble de nouveaux troubles. Et toujours ces sortes de *gifles dans le mental*.

Tout en réfléchissant, et tâchant – plus difficile – de mettre mes réflexions en ligne, je m'étais déjà vingt fois, ou quinze au moins, moliéresquement insulté en paroles: «Quel imbécile j'avais été d' avaler, sans le moindre essai préliminaire, une forte dose de ce produit inconnu qu'on m'avait donné comme très bon, c'est-à-dire très actif. Ridicule! Inacceptable ridicule!»

Cependant les troubles du mécanisme mettaient en route sans répit les oppositions, les contradictions, sapaient tout et n'importe quoi et constamment de manière que, manipulés en tous sens, les faits apparemment les mieux enregistrés, les plus récents, n'avaient plus de réalité.

Après une dizaine de retours en arrière, la réalité, on ne l'apercevait plus; en tant que certitude, elle n'existait plus.

Plus je réfléchissais, plus je provoquais une circulation défectueuse.

Plus je cherchais à me rappeler clairement un fait, plus vite je le retrouvais non avenu. À l'affirmation inéluctablement se substituait la négation, sans que j'y fusse pour rien. S'agissait-il d'impulsions hors de mon contrôle? Propriétaire du mécanisme pensant, j'observais et je l'observais. Opposition – affirmation, entre ces deux pôles contraires il devenait impossible de prendre parti.

waves come over me, I lose it.

Assaults on the centres of balance. How many such centres there are! And how many where one never expected them to be!

Dislocations. All the strength gone out of my mental grip. I wasn't expecting that. That is something new.

I lie down. Useless. The couch, as though no longer a couch, ..., rests me for not one second. As well stretch out on a spade or a rake. At least let us take advantage of this condition. I can observe the processes of the brain more closely, the way it continues to reason point by point, as if nothing were wrong, and constantly plays over the facts still in its possession. Oh, logic, unruffled logic, still putting things together and getting nowhere and going on bravely nevertheless, unfailingly piling error upon error. What a sight!

I am a long way off understanding and appreciating exactly what it is that has been unsettled in me and what is upsetting me now with new upheavals. And these continual *slaps in the mind*, if I can call them that.

Whilst thinking and – a more difficult matter – trying to put my thoughts in order, I had twenty times, or fifteen at least, already hurled insults at myself in the manner of a character in Molière: What a fool I was to take such a large dose of an unknown substance said to be very good – that is, very effective – when it was given to me And without trying it out at all first! Ridiculous! An unforgiveable folly!

Meanwhile the upset mechanism went on remorselessly instigating contradictions and opposition, undermined anything and everything and all the time in such a way that things apparently best, because most recently, registered, being pushed and pulled in all directions, lost their reality.

Reality, after being set back a dozen times, was no longer able to be perceived; as something certain, it had ceased to exist.

The harder I thought, the more defectively my reasoning proceeded.

The harder I tried to remember any fact clearly, the sooner I found that it woud not come. Anything affirmed would be inevitably negated, without my having any part in the process. Were they impulses over which I had no control? The thinking mechanism was mine: I was the observer, I was observing it. Opposition-affirmation: between those two contrary poles it was becoming impossible to choose.

Ainsi le fait indéniable entre tous, origine et source de mes maux présents, celui de la découverte fortuite et de l'absorption précipitée de la drogue, après nombre de manipulations, substitutions, inversions, interversions et contradictions, je ne savais plus s'il avait eu lieu. Un extrême et actif imbroglio s'y était substitué où vérité et fausseté également importantes revenaient en retournements incessants.

Et si c'était faux cela, me disais-je, cette soi-disant absorption de drogue? Cela sent vraiment trop l'histoire inventée après coup. Ce paquet retrouvé après des années, dans un tiroir, pas même caché, et cependant échappant à la vue, et dont je me serais emparé et servi à l'instant. Pourquoi à l'instant, alors que depuis longtemps je n'en avais plus aucune envie? Ma présente crise (?) pouvait être simplement un fort malaise comme il peut en arriver, une excitation, bouffée délirante ou quelque chose de ce genre, causé par l'insomnie, l'épuisement.

– Et le détail alors?

– Mais justement, les détails constituent le signe même de l'invention, du faux, de la vraisemblance cherchée à tout prix, lorsque le fait manque de fondement réel... D'ailleurs je n'arrive même pas à retrouver le nom de la voyageuse qui m'aurait fait ce détestable cadeau et à un âge si peu propice à ces expériences... d'ailleurs abandonnées depuis bientôt un quart de siècle.

À y réfléchir des jours plus tard, d'abord le fait de l'absorption aurait été sapé, défait, puis le fait de son activité, puis le fait de la découverte même du produit, puis le fait du tiroir où il aurait été retrouvé...

Une pensée tâtonnante et incidente, de celles qu'on a autour d'un sujet me serait venue à l'esprit comme: «*Ah si je pouvais seulement avoir imaginé ce qui m'arrive...*» et au lieu de n'être et de ne rester qu'un désir, qu'un vague et vain regret se serait par suite des présents renforcements ensuite présentée sous la forme: «Ce qui est arrivé, c'est de l'imagination.» Car les phrases, les pensées même, avaient couramment dans cet état une structure mécanique, rigide, et des déplacements pareils, tandis que les sentiments, ici le doute, m'échappaient. J'observais les difficultés auxquelles avait à faire, fort à faire, cette nouvelle résultante que j'étais devenu.

. . . .

Thus the one fact undeniable among all others, the origin and source of my present ills, the fact of the chance discovery of the drug and my hastily swallowing it, after numerous acts of manipulation, substitution, inversion, transposition and contradiction, I no longer knew if it had ever happened. In its place was an extreme and potent confusion where truth and untruth, in equal measure, came and went and came again incessantly.

And what if it were untrue, I said to myself, and I never did swallow any drug? The whole thing sounds too much like a story made up after the event. The packet discovered after so many years, in a drawer, not even hidden, and yet never noticed before, and immediately taken up and used... And why immediately when for so long I had had no interest in such things? My present crisis (?) might be no more than that I was feeling ill, over-excited, giddy, some common thing of that nature brought on by lack of sleep or exhaustion.
– And what about the details?
– But it is precisely the details which indicate that a thing is invented, untrue, and that the *appearance* of truth is being striven for at any price, the facts themselves having no foundation in reality... Besides, I cannot even remember what that woman travelling was called who is supposed to have given me the wretched substance, and at an age so ill-suited to such experiments... which I had, moreover, given up a quarter of a century before.

Reflecting on it some days later, what was first undermined and undone was the fact of my having taken the drug, then the fact of its effects, then of my discovering it in the first place, then the fact of the drawer in which it had been found...
Or a thought occurred to me, one among many the subject might provoke, one hesitant and incidental thought, such as: '*Oh, if only I had only imagined what is happening to me...*' and instead of being and remaining merely a wish, the vague and vain regret, as a result of receiving reinforcement in the present, subsequently presented itself to me thus: 'What has happened was all imagined.' For in that state my sentences and even my thoughts were for the most part structured mechanically and rigidly, and displacement followed accordingly; whereas my feelings – in this case doubt – eluded me. I noted the difficulties which I – or the new thing I had become – was having, very urgently, to deal with.

. . . .

Et si tout de même je m'efforçais de vérifier? À la cuisine, lieu de préparation du produit absorbé, devaient subsister des restes de l'opération; s'il y avait une chance pour que tout soit inventé, je le saurais. Les traces ou l'absence de traces en décideront. Et je me lève, déclenchant ainsi de nouveaux troubles et les mêmes questions pour la cinquantième fois sur ce qui s'est réellement passé.

Franchir la porte, quel problème dans l'état où je suis! Il ne faut pas que je me trompe, que je fasse l'inverse, qu'au lieu d'ouvrir, ou bien après avoir ouvert, que je ferme, que je m'enferme. J'essaie, laissant la première porte largement ouverte, puis poussant la deuxième, et attention à la suivante, la porte donnant sur le palier, si je la laisse ouverte, le concierge étant souvent dans l'escalier, il ne faut pas qu'il entre et me voie dans cet état, marchant à pas incertains, s'il me questionne, plus probablement je parlerai de travers sans trouver les mots, même les principaux, de ceux qu'il n'est pas d'un homme normal d'oublier.

Sautant d'un projet à l'autre, je tente d'écrire sur un carton le *nom* d'un ami pour lui téléphoner éventuellement. Je ne retrouve pas l'orthographe. J'essaye de prononcer son nom. Ma façon laborieuse de le prononcer (ce nom ou un autre) me rendrait suspect, ce ne doit pas être ainsi que je fais d'habitude. Cela me ferait du bien pourtant, si lui et moi, on se disait quelques mots. Les miens, même incorrects, il les prendrait peut-être pour une plaisanterie.

Cependant, la marche que j'entreprenais, plus ou moins oubliée, laissée de côté par l'inadvertance, reste arrêtée. Ma tête seule demeure pleine de marches, de projets, de représentations de marche. En vue de quelle fin? Je ne sais plus. Un témoin qui me verrait penserait que je ne sais pas me conduire! Ah cela revient, le bout manquant se présente et je me remets en route. Mais à mi-chemin, ne dépassant pas l'entrée et loin encore du but, ne sachant plus pour quelle raison je suis là, je renonce et reviens à la chambre sans avoir rien vérifié.

Les schémas opératoires surtout manquent. Et quelle affaire aussi que de décider! D'avoir à se décider à être ici, plutôt que là… ou au-delà encore ou au-delà, et de, constamment, tenir ensemble tous les éléments du «plan». Car le moindre déplacement je le vois, en comporte un. Mais je ne l'aperçois que fugitivement.

All the same, supposing I forced myself to check? In the kitchen, where I had prepared the substance I then swallowed, there must still be the leftovers of the operation; I should be able to find out if it was possible that the whole thing had been invented. There will be traces or there will not be traces, and that will decide. And I get to my feet, which occasions further confusion and the same questions for the fiftieth time as to what has really happened.

What a problem it is to get through the door in the state I am in! I must not do the wrong thing, not do the opposite and instead of opening the door, or having opened it, close it and shut myself in. I try, leaving the first door wide open, and pushing open the second and now careful with the next, the door that gives on to the landing, if I leave that one open I do not want the concierge – who is often on the stairs – to come in and see me in this state, walking uncertainly, if he questions me I'll be sure to answer him oddly and not find the words, even the main ones a normal person does not usually forget.

Rapidly moving from one plan to another I attempt to write on a piece of cardboard the *name* of a friend, to telephone him, possibly. I can't remember how to spell it. I try to pronounce his name. My laborious way of pronouncing it (this name or any other) would arouse suspicion, that cannot be the way I usually say it. And yet it would do me good if he and I were to exchange a few words. He would take mine, in their disorder, as a joke perhaps.

Meanwhile I had almost forgotten having set off towards the kitchen. My journey there had been abandoned, for want of attention. Only my head remains full of such journeys, projects, ideas of setting off. With what end in view? I no longer know. Anyone seeing me now would think I was not in control of myself. But then it comes back, what was missing comes back, and I set off again. But halfway there, getting no further than the door of the flat and still some distance from my destination, I give up, no longer knowing why I am there, and go back to the bedroom without checking anything.

I particularly lack any system. And what a business it is, besides, to make any decision! To have to decide to be in this place rather than that… or perhaps over there, or there, and constantly to have to hold together all the elements of "the plan". For I see that the least displacement necessitates a plan. But this is only fleetingly apparent.

Lassitude, vertige, impression que je m'enfermais, que j'allais m'enfermer, que le gardien alerté... mais comment?

Dans la drogue, le danger, c'est l'acte.
Se tromper dans la formation et l'énoncé des pensées, soit. Mais se tromper d'acte, c'est grave et immédiatement. Je le vois. L'avais-je oublié?

Autre mauvaise surprise, qu'en effet je n'avais pas eue avant: *ces oublis* de toutes parts et à toute minute.
Ce serait bien l'effet de ma faiblissante mémoire (pourquoi pas?) qui, depuis des années, devenue mon point faible et à surveiller, a pu dans l'état présent avoir été attaquée particulièrement et rendue plus déficiente. Défaillance sur défaillances. Je n'avais pas prévu cette supplémentaire diminution et les déconnexions trop nombreuses qui allaient s'ensuivre...

Après nombre de tiraillements, efforts et arrêts, je me retrouve dans l'atelier; *mon* atelier? Atelier?

Si je m'étais trouvé à un quatre-vingt-dixième étage, vitres cassées, un jour d'ouragan, mes papiers emportés par dizaines de feuilles, la paperasse en trombe attirée au-dehors, tourbillonnant autour de moi, courbé, à demi aveuglé, en même temps qu'interpelle en langue étrangère...
C'était quelque chose comme ça, mon état... (état!), oui, mais dans l'abstrait, sans quoi que ce soit de concret ou de figuré.

Apathie d'autre part, en quelque autre part, et encore autre part, et démantèlement. Conjointement, un dehors quasi imperturbé, sans l'ombre d'un souffle.
Mais j'étais poussé. Oh comme j'étais poussé!
Et on peut l'être phénoménalement. J'en étais assommé. Poussées invisibles contre lesquelles je me tends et me serre. Sollicitations continuelles, auxquelles je résiste. Non je n'accepte pas de me jeter du haut de ce balcon. D'un quatrième étage, ce serait idiot.
Poussée aussitôt repoussée, aussitôt revenue, et pas de temps pour l'examen des suites probables et leur discussion.

Dans cet état on ne voit pas les conséquences. Elles ne viennent pas en rang vous renseigner, elles aussi interrompues, hachées, et

Fatigue, dizziness, the feeling that I was shutting myself in, that I was about to shut myself in, and that the caretaker, having been alerted... but how?

With drugs the dangerous thing is action.

It is all very well to make a mistake in forming and uttering your thoughts; but to make a mistake in what you do, is serious and immediately so. I am aware of that. Had I forgotten it?

Another unpleasant surprise, something new in fact: *these lapses of memory* everywhere and every minute.

Doubtless a result of my failing memory (why not?) which, having been for years my weak point and something I have to watch, must now in this present state have been especially badly affected and rendered still more deficient. Failure upon failure. I had not anticipated this further diminution and the countless disconnections that would ensue...

After much agonising and numerous stops and starts I find myself back in the studio; *my* studio? Studio?

If I had found myself on the ninetieth floor somewhere, with broken windows in a hurricane, and all my papers blowing away in sheaves, sucked into space and whirling around me, and I was bowed, half-blinded and being questioned meanwhile in a foreign tongue...

Yes, the state I was in (state!) was something like that... but in the abstract, with nothing in the least concrete or visual about it.

Otherwise apathy, in some other place, in yet another place, and a dismantling. And at the same time an exterior that was all unperturbed, scarcely ruffled.

But I was driven! Oh how I was driven!

Unbelievable, to what degree a person may be impelled. I was assailed by impulses – by invisible forces against which I tensed and clenched myself. Repeated demands, which I resisted. No, I refuse to throw myself off the balcony. From the fourth floor it would be an idiotic thing to do.

An impulse no sooner repelled, it returns at once, leaving no time to examine and discuss the probable consequences.

In that state it is not possible to see the consequences. They do not line up to tell you what they are, they are themselves sporadic

pas d'évocation ou courte, et genre «épure», inémotive et qui ne compte pas, où l'idée des souffrances ne prend pas un aspect imaginatif et dramatique. Il faut pourtant s'accrocher à quelque chose, faire surgir un accident tout en repoussant la pensée maraudeuse, débordante de tentations. Intensément quelque chose en soi cherche l'acte libérateur, la libératrice minute – fatale peut-être – sans s'occuper de ce qui va suivre.

Il me faut donc condamner la vue du balcon, de peur qu'attiré je m'y trouve, soudain l'enjambant, conscient trop tard, déjà me basculant dans le vide.

Faire attention. Attention à ne pas se laisser aller. Suicides par inattention. Dans la drogue, que de suicides d'«absents», de distraits.

Morts par manque de vigilance.

Non, ce n'est pas le moment de se laisser aller. Il s'agit de tenir un certain temps – deux heures ou trois ou quatre, après lesquelles le plus dur sans doute sera passe... si j'arrive jusque-là.

L'avenir, qu'est-ce qui m'en reste?

Essayons de voir clair dans le temps.

Par les calculs, les erreurs sur le temps allaient commencer. C'est à cinq heures, si vraiment elle avait eu lieu, que l'opération avait débuté. Même si elle n'avait pas eu réellement lieu, quand j'entrai dans l'atelier et vis de façon si stimulée, si exceptionnelle, dessins, photos et peintures qui s'y trouvaient... il était cinq heures vingt. Surpris que «ça parte si vite» et pris d'un vieux réflexe de séances mescaliniennes d'autrefois j'avais consulté ma montre à deux ou trois reprises.

C'était parti à ce moment, moment de la déchirure, de quoi la mémoire garde une marque.

Depuis, que de choses, de pertes de choses, de retournements de choses! Il a dû se passer deux heures, ou deux heures et demie alors qu'à ma montre... Non ce n'est pas possible il ne se serait réellement passé que vingt-trois ou vingt-cinq minutes. Une nouvelle confrontation s'impose. J'attends – avec peine – trois quarts d'heure ou une bonne demi-heure sûrement, avant de consulter ma montre à nouveau et le cadran d'un réveil. À les en croire, il ne se serait passé que trois minutes! ou trois minutes et demie!

and in pieces, they evoke nothing, or only briefly, sketchily, unemotively, they hardly count, in them the idea of a painful outcome does not take on any imaginative or dramatic form. And yet it is necessary to keep hold of something, conjure up an accident even as you push away the thought that has waylaid you with an abundance of temptations. Intensely something within you is seeking the liberating act, the liberating moment – fatal perhaps – and is careless of what will follow.

I must therefore block out the sight of the balcony for fear that I might be drawn to it and suddenly find myself astride it, conscious too late, and already toppling into the void.

Be careful. Careful not to let go. Suicide through a lack of attention. With drugs, how many kill themselves absent-mindedly, not really there.

Dead through a lack of vigilance.

No, this is not the moment to let oneself go. Hold on for a while – two hours or three or four, after which the worst will surely be over... if I make it till then.

The future: what is there left of it for me?

Let us try to look clearly at time.

Beginning my calculations, that was the beginning of my errors about time. If it took place at all, then the whole affair had begun at five o'clock. And even if it never did take place, when I went into the studio and saw in such a heightened and unwonted fashion the drawings, photographs and paintings there... that was at twenty past five. Surprised to have "begun" so quickly and acting on an old reflex from my mescalin sessions I had looked at my watch two or three times.

It had begun at that moment, the moment of rift, which impresses itself upon the memory.

So many things since then, things lost, things turned upside down. Two hours must have elapsed or two and a half... whereas my watch... Am I to believe that in reality only twenty-three or twenty-five minutes have elapsed? I will do the comparison again. I wait – with difficulty – three quarters of an hour or at least a good half hour before looking at my watch and the dial of an alarm clock. If I am to believe them only three minutes have passed! or three and a half!

À ce compte, fâcheusement approximatif et continuellement changeant, c'est bien cinquante heures, ou soixante ou quatre-vingts ou cent des miennes que je vais devoir tenir (heures qu'en îlots de trois ou quatre minutes je vais désespérément trouver à ma montre) avant de pouvoir rencontrer un mieux...

je n'arriverai jamais au bout.

À partir de là, je me suis mis à me frapper, à me pincer, à m' asperger d'eau froide... piètres interventions.

Courts répits. Si je n'arrête pas le processus dévastateur, du moins je le ralentis.

. . . .

... Trop faibles, les coups. Il faut que je me fasse plus mal à la tête, à la poitrine, au ventre. Je masse et frappe la nuque et le pied je le tords. Heureusement j'ai une sorte d'abcès au pied. Heurter la table et le divan le réveillent, me réveillent pour de courts moments. Un mauvais «je ne sais quoi» m'atterre. Du neutre, un large neutre se dilate et tend à m'assujettir. À cause de quoi je dois veiller.

Après une séance de coups... épuisé, je m'étends. Ce ne sont que deux minutes de gagnées, puis deux encore. Il faut continuer, ce que je fais de façon sans doute risible... mais qui me permet de résister. Si insuffisants que soient les coups, j'ai quand même mis un poids, un contrepoids sur la balance où mon moi et ma volonté ne pesions quasiment plus rien.

L'esprit d'observation, le pouvoir de séparation, d'analyse partiellement «revenus».

Fausse joie. Je le reperds. Il est reperdu.

Toujours dans le brouhaha. Au milieu du tourbillon, des tourbillons, dans une place sans place, que des salves d'obnubilations interrompent.

Pourquoi le mur d'en face n'est-il plus entièrement un mur? Pourquoi? Mur sans les propriétés de mur. Lesquelles? Accoutumé à un certain taux de matérialité, de dureté, de raideur en lui..., que je ne serais plus à même de suffisamment ressentir ni d'évoquer. Car pour ce qui est d'apercevoir le mur et les choses, je les vois sans distorsion appréciable.

By that reckoning, which is tiresomely approximate and constantly shifting, it is at least fifty hours or sixty or eighty or a hundred of mine that I am going to have to endure (hours which I shall find on my watch in little islands of three or four minutes) before I can begin to feel any improvement...

I shall never get there.

From that moment I began slapping, pinching and splashing myself with cold water... pathetic measures.

Brief respites. If I cannot halt the process of destruction, at least I can slow it down.

. . . .

... The blows are too slight. I need to give myself greater pain, in the head, the chest, the belly. I squeeze and slap the nape of my neck and twist at my foot. Luckily I have a sort of abcess on the foot. Banging against the table and the couch revives it and revives me, briefly. Something sinister, something I cannot give a name to, lays me low. A blankness, a vast blankness dilates and threatens to overwhelm me. For that reason I must stay awake.

Having spent some time hitting myself... I lie down, exhausted. I have only gained two minutes, then two more. I must carry on, and I do, in a manner which is doubtless ridiculous... but which enables me to resist. The blows are inadequate, of course, but I have nevertheless placed a weight, a counterweight, on the scales where my self and my will were weighing almost nothing.

My powers of observation, the ability to discriminate and analyse, have partially "returned".

I rejoice too soon. I am losing them again... They are lost.

Still in the hubbub. In the midst of the whirlwind, of whirlwinds, in a place without location assailed repeatedly by my obsessions.

Why is the wall opposite no longer entirely a wall? Why? A wall without the properties of a wall. And which? Being used to a certain degree of materiality, of hardness, stiffness in a wall..., am I now perhaps no longer capable of either feeling it sufficiently or of evoking it? For as to *seeing* the wall and other objects, that I can do without any appreciable distortion.

La chambre, dirai-je, manque de *conclusion*.

Ce n'est pas dans une chambre de biais ou penchée le moins du monde que je me trouve. Et le «vertige», si vertige il y eut, est passé. Dérangement plus fin est celui à cause de quoi je n'arrive plus à *savoir ce mur pareil*, quoique inchangé en apparence. «Atteint en son être», un mur sans son physique. Mur non enrobé *dans sa muralité*.

Un mur que je voudrais rétablir, et que je souffre de ne pas parvenir à rétablir.

Est-ce tellement indispensable? Il semble.

Une sorte de défection de l'élémentaire par suite d'une défection du métaphysique, ou une défection du métaphysique par suite d'une défection de l'élémentaire, ou défections à ce double niveau sans que l'une soit cause de l'autre, mais parallèlement *se* et *me* défaisant...

Dans ce trouble s'approfondissant et s'étageant et où ce remuement à la fois m'étale et me soustrait, et défait les hiérarchies, rien n'est sûr.

Concepts dépassés.

Presque tout maintenant a tendance (c'est mon «donné» actuel) à être également acceptable et inacceptable, jamais définitivement inadmissible (valeur qui n'existe plus). Accepter, non accepter: des *mesures que je ne prends plus*. Ce qu'il y aurait (et avait) d'inconciliable dans *ici* qui serait *là*, dans *avant* qui se passerait *après*, ou dans un carré simultanément et également cercle, et généralement les concepts excluant un concept opposé, c'est cela qui n'est plus, qui ne se présente plus. L'idée et son contraire, l'une et l'autre également injustifiables, indécidables.

Les catégories ont perdu toute force. Elles n'existent pas *sans autorité*. Celle-ci devait me manquer sans que je la sente me manquer. Cela devait se passer plus profond, là où le sentiment n'a pas accès.

De tout, du plus physique, l'être amenuisé ne reçoit que du métaphysique.

Du métaphysique réel, vécu, subi, expérimental auquel on a directement affaire, pas tiré d'enseignement livresque ou d'un sujet discuté et rediscuté entre collègues, mais d'un «indéfiniss-

The bedroom, in my view, lacks *conclusion.*

Not that I am in a room that slants or is the least bit sloping. And my "dizziness", if it was dizziness, has gone. A subtler disruption is the one on account of which I can no longer manage *to know the wall is the same wall*, for all that its appearance is unchanged. "Afflicted in its very being", a wall without its physical self. A wall no longer clothed *in its wallness.*

A wall I should like to reinstate, and which I grieve at not being able to reinstate.

Is it so very necessary? It would seem to be.

A sort of failure in the physical world as a consequence of a failure in the metaphysical, or a failure of the metaphysical world as a consequence of a failure in the physical, or failures on both levels without either being the cause of the other, but simultaneously undoing *themselves* and *me...*

In this confusion as it deepens and as it rises and whose movement both extends and diminishes me and undoes all the hierarchies, nothing is sure.

Outmoded concepts.

Almost everything now tends (this constitutes my present starting point) to be acceptable and unacceptable in equal measure, never definitely inadmissible (a category which has ceased to exist). To accept or not to accept: these are *courses I no longer pursue.* What would be (and was) irreconcilable in *here* being *there*, in a *before* taking place *after*, or in a square being simultaneously and equally a circle, and generally concepts which exclude an opposite concept, that is what no longer obtains, no longer presents itself. The idea and its opposite, each equally unable to be justified or decided.

The categories have lost their force. *Without authority* they do not exist. It must be authority I'm lacking, without feeling that I am lacking it. This must be happening at some deeper level, to which the feelings do not have access.

From everything, from the most physical things, what comes to me in my diminished state is only the metaphysical.

The metaphysical world – real, lived, suffered, experimental – dealt with direct, not drawn from any bookish learning or from a topic discussed and discussed again among colleagues, but drawn from

able» où on a abordé, pénétré et dont on est pénétré, où plus ou moins l'on risque sa tête, dans une autre étendue. Il s'agit d'un illimité intrinsèque, d'un illimitable.

Ce *physique* passé à un *paraphysique* et dont on n'oublie pas le danger est pour cela ressenti comme pénible et accompagné d'une impression odieuse, inhumaine. Est-ce pour y résister, par moments, que je me tiens les yeux et la pensée fixés sur le mur d'en face (sur sa partie nue, dégagée), mur qui a fait ses preuves comme mur, comme solide, comme têtu, comme invariant, comme résistant à être tantôt ceci, tantôt cela, un mur que rien ne tient, dont cependant la dureté n'est plus pareille. Elle manque et me manque.

Le *réel* – le tenu pour réel, qui serait réel même pour un chien, – manque en ce moment, continue à *manquer* par vagues.
Le mur sans sa nature de mur, c'est incroyablement éprouvant. Homme ou animal, on doit pouvoir compter sur les solides.

Le temps (autre sujet d'alerte) n'avance toujours pas comme il fait d'habitude, charriant posément des masses d'impressions communes, le temps comme il est *établi* en nous.
Il ne fait pas de cadeaux, ce temps, ou seulement de plus subtils, que je n'aperçois qu'à peine, ne saisis pas, ne saurais saisir, encore moins utiliser.

Je répète beaucoup. Par répétitions sans doute fallait-il alors absolument empêcher la zone neutre – et balayeuse – de gagner et d'entraîner d'autres zones encore intactes. Le terrain encore quadrillé ne devrait pas perdre de son quadrillage.

Résistance difficile, longue encore, longue. Je n'en peux plus d'attendre que le temps à ma montre se remette à avancer conformément au mien où je circule à une autre allure, mais c'est ma montre qui, inversement, me paraît ralentir, être en défaut, s'attarder indûment, n'ayant point place pour mes péripéties, ne consommant que quelques minutes, là où je vis une aventure des heures durant, des heures pleines de risques.

Cela ne peut se prolonger. Je ne veux plus de ce temps traînard qui ne fait pas de cas du mien, écart intolérable.

something "indefinable" where we have made a start and entered it and had it enter us, more or less risking our necks in another dimension. It is something intrinsically unlimited, unable to be limited.

This *physical condition* having passed into a *paraphysical* one and its dangerous nature not having been forgotten is for that reason felt to be painful and the impression it makes is hateful and inhuman. Perhaps in order to resist it, occasionally, I fix my eyes and my thoughts on the wall opposite (where it is bare and exposed), a wall which has proved itself as a wall, proved itself solid, obstinate, unvarying, resistant to being now this, now that, a wall that is subject to nothing, whose hardness is nevertheless now no longer what it was. That hardness is missing and I miss it.

The *real* – what is held to be real and what would be real even for a dog – is missing at this moment and in waves continues *to be missing*.
The wall not having the nature of a wall is unbelievably distressing.
Man or animal, we need to be able to rely on things being solid.

Time (another cause for alarm) is still not going forward as it normally does, steadily conveying our masses of common impressions, time as it is established in us.
The time I am in gives nothing away: or its gifts are of so subtle a kind that I barely notice, fail to grasp, am incapable of grasping and even less capable of using them.

I repeat myself a good deal. Then, no doubt, repetition was absolutely necessary to prevent the blank – and overwhelming – zone from reaching and carrying away with it other zones still intact. The terrain then still under some formal control must not be allowed to lose it.

A difficult resistance, long, still long. I am weary of waiting for the time by my watch to begin moving forward again in accordance with the time which *I* inhabit and in which I travel at a different pace; but in fact my watch seems to be slowing down, to be going wrong, to be unconscionably slow, and not to be ample enough to contain my wanderings, for it eats up a few little minutes whilst I am living through an adventure lasting hours, hours full of risk.

This can't go on. I am sick of this slowcoach time which disregards my time, the gap between them is intolerable.

Je me décide à prendre un tranquillisant, un comprimé.

Je n'ai pourtant pas oublié qu'à certains malades, à des mélancoliques c'est ce calmant même qui fit leur perte.

Les débarrassant de leur incertitude, de leurs hésitations, de leur peur, il les avait conduits au suicide en suspendant leur irrésolution.

Absence courte, pas nulle.

Je m'intéresse moins au mur, au problème qu'il présentait.

Après un autre intervalle, lorsque je regardai la paroi à nouveau, ce n'était plus du même œil. Y avait-il eu du changement?

Six heures vingt-cinq. Presque une demi-heure de passée.

Mon temps ralentissait, se rapprochait de l'autre.

Pris un second comprimé.

Étirement somnolant.

J'ai donc pu reposer; oui cela commençait à ressembler à du repos. J'étais sur le chemin. Quand je consultai ma montre elle avait réappris *mon* temps. Nous doublions le cap des sept heures. Sauvetage en vue...

J'avais évité le pire. Je n'avais pas tout à fait été renversé. Je peux reposer, accepter de reposer...

et je n'ai appelé personne, personne n'a su.

. . . .

Je venais de connaître encore un inconnaissable, un tout autre non promis à ma nature, dommage – plutôt assommé qu'éclairé. Observer de l'apathie avec de l'apathie, pas facile. Hésitant, perplexe (ce degré de perplexité m'était inconnu).

S'aggrave une difficulté à trouver les mots. Les mots à écrire.

Ce récit, à se former, comme il traînait, comme nous avons traîné ensemble.

I decide to take a tranquilliser.

Not that I have forgotten that for some sufferers, for depressives, it was the calmant itself which brought about their downfall.

Freeing them of their uncetainty, their hesitations, their fear, it led them into suicide by suspending their inability to decide.

A brief absence, not to be despised.

I am less interested in the wall, in the problem it posed.

After another interval, when I looked at the wall again it was no longer with the same eyes. Had there been a change?

Six twenty-five. Nearly half an hour gone by.

My time was slowing down, getting nearer the other.

Took a second tablet.

Sleepy stretching.

So I was able to rest; yes, it began to resemble rest. I was on the way. When I looked at my watch it had learned *my* time again. We were rounding the cape of seven o'clock. Rescue in sight...

I had avoided the worst. I had not been completely overthrown. I can rest, I can allow myself to rest...

nor did I call anyone, nobody knew.

. . . .

I had just made the acquaintance of another unknowable thing, something quite other and not intended for my nature, a pity – I was stunned rather than illuminated. To observe apathy apathetically is not easy. Hesitant, perplexed (that degree of perplexity was unknown to me).

Increasingly difficult to find the words. The words to write.

How slow this account was to take shape, how slowly we dragged along.

Lendemains

Le monde est redevenu extérieur, bien extérieur, exclusif, nettement partagé en catégories.

Le chatouillis des lumières, des sons, des couleurs est là, avec leurs renseignements habituels. Surfaces, surfaces, pas de danger qu'on les traverse, qu'on soit en elles ou elles en vous. Faites pour rester superficielles, aux émissions superficielles pour capteurs superficiels.

L'étrange est qu'il soit redevenu si peu étrange, si fréquentable, commode, aisé à reconnaître, à décoder.

J'ai mis six mois à écrire ce peu de pages. Je n'avais pris aucune note. Désirant solliciter ma mémoire pour quelques indications, je rentrai petit à petit dans le souvenir de cela que je ne sais toujours comment nommer, avec quoi bon gré mal gré j'avais dû vivre, refusant l'alliance, où tout de même je restais pris.

Même les personnes les plus proches ne furent au courant de rien. D'avoir à me taire, à garder le secret contribua à préserver les restes à demi endormis de l'événement.

J'avais reçu en cette après-midi, qui disposa de moi, le grand cadeau d'un autre monde. J'y avais abordé et il m'avait enveloppé, m'avait inclus.

Terra incognita.

Domaine dont même tout près on perd les limites, qui fondent.

Domaine qui ne se livre qu'à l'indigent, subtilement, essentiellement démuni, ayant fait abandon, fût-ce d'abord malgré lui, des saveurs et micro-saveurs élémentaires et dans une ascèse cherchée ou non recherchée, mais acceptée, fait abandon de ses armes et de ses défenses journalières. Au dépourvu seulement en pouvoirs de compartimentage, le monde vient, unique, incomparable au-delà des troubles, toujours le dépassant.

Monde aimanté, dont lorsqu'il n'en reste plus rien on sent encore la dense absence.

Mornings after

The world has become external again, very external, exclusive, neatly divided into categories.

The stimuli of light, sound, colour are there, imparting the usual information. Surfaces, surfaces, no danger of passing through them and being in them or they in you. They are made to remain superficial, to transmit superficialities for superficial receivers.

The strange thing is that the world has become so very *un*strange again, so easy to be in, manageable, easy to recognise and decode.

It has taken me six months to write these few pages. I had not made any notes. In consulting my memory for a few clues I returned little by little into a recollection of the condition I still cannot give a name to, in which, like it or not, I had been obliged to live, resisting the association which bound me nevertheless.

Even those closest to me knew nothing about it. Being obliged to keep silent, to keep the secret, helped preserve what had not yet disappeared of the event.

That afternoon, which did as it liked with me, I had been given the great gift of another world. I had landed there, it had enfolded and included me.

Terra incognita.

A land whose boundaries, even close to, are easily lost: they melt away.

A land which bestows itself only on the needy, the subtly and essentially unprovided man who has relinquished, perhaps at first despite himself, all the elementary flavours and micro-flavours and in an asceticism either sought or not sought but accepted, relinquishes his everyday arms and defences. Only to the man deprived of his powers of compartmentalisation does that world come, unique, incomparable, beyond his confusions, always exceeding him. A magnetic world which even when it has entirely gone leaves behind a palpable dense absence.

*

Avec une autre vue tel sujet se confrontant autrement pourrait se considérer ainsi: comme partagé par le fait de l'accident en zones nouvelles de conscience et d'inconscience, aussi bien l'une que l'autre,

ces niveaux et provinces qu'il découvre, dont une sorte d'infini est le compagnon et le fond fuyant, seraient le plus souvent les strates quasi sans fin de son évolution à rebours qu'il remonte, pas seulement celle de sa personne, mais de l'espèce humaine en lui; retombé, en bien des points, à l'antérieur, à l'arrière, avec alors des fonctions inachevées, nues, primitives. Et l'enrichissant manchon de concomitantes perceptions-impressions acquises au long des âges alors faisant défaut... et le désorientant.

*

Another observer from another point of view confronting himself in a different manner might see himself thus: as being divided by the fact of the accident into new zones of consciousness and unconsciousness, the one as much as the other,

these levels and regions he discovers, whose accompaniment and shifting background is a sort of infinity, are they not most often the seemingly endless strata of a contrary evolution through which he regresses? – not only his but that of the human race in him; thrown back, in several respects, into what is prior and arrested, with functions then correspondingly imperfect, naked, primitive. And what he acquired in passing through the ages, an attendant wealth of perceptions-impressions, it loses its luminance... he loses his whereabouts.

Le jardin exalté

The heavenly garden

Il restait un peu du produit préparé, lorsque quelques jours plus tard, on me proposa un jardin à la campagne. Quelqu'un voulait faire un essai.

Dose faible, endroit calme, ciel dégagé. La personne avait préparé quelques disques. Au dernier moment elle montra de l'appréhension.

Pour ma part, je commence mal: des serrements de cœur. Décidément devenu impropre à ces experiences.

Sur elle, l'effet est bon. Une heureuse surprise remplace l'inquiétude et les traits tirés.

Intéressée, elle prend part, distingue, surveille, décrit à voix murmurée les transformations, de la zone visuelle surtout, creux et plis dans un tableau ou au mur.
Les lointains dans le fond du jardin se laissent davantage apercevoir, «semblent, dit-elle, vouloir attirer l'attention».

Lit-elle dans ma pensée, comme elle dira bientôt, ou moi sans rien dire dans la sienne? Est-ce l'accroissement simultané de finesse de la perception oculaire, chez elle comme chez moi, qui soudainement et donc comme exprès paraît désigner des détails jusque-là non remarqués?

Apaisée, elle donne ses impressions. C'est la détente, confiance revenue. Le visage aussi le dit, moins que ses paroles, moins longtemps, plus réfléchi; changeant. Il semble pour les expressions, doué nouvellement; comme soumis à une manipulation. Témoin de ce à quoi l'organisme est soumis, mis à l'épreuve, à différentes épreuves et différents niveaux, par différents organes successivement.

Visage en difficulté, en traitement, intérieurement travaillé. Des paroles cependant paisibles continuent à en partir: Discordances tantôt légères, tantôt fort singulières.
À une remarque prudente que je fais à ce sujet, elle se révèle grandement surprise. Ainsi elle n'est pas au courant! Elle ignore

There was still a little of the substance left made up when, a few days later, it was suggested I might try a garden in the country. Somebody wanted to experiment.

A small dose, a quiet place, clear skies. The person in question had assembled some records. At the last minute she began to be apprehensive.

As for me, I got off to a bad start: a tightness around the heart. Clearly I'm no longer up to these adventures.

But the effect on her is a good one. Her anxiety gives way to a feeling of happy surprise; her features relax.

She becomes engaged, things interest her, she distinguishes them, they come under her gaze, in a murmuring voice she describes the transformations, above all visual, hollows and folds in a picture or in the wall.
The depths of the garden become more perceptible, they seem, as she says, to be attracting her attention.

Can she read my thoughts, as she will claim to before long, or can I, without saying a word, read hers? Is it the simultaneous heightening of visual perception, in her and in me, which suddenly, and thus as if deliberately, seems to highlight details unnoticed before now?

Quietened, she gives her impressions. Relaxation, the return of confidence. Her face expresses it too, but less than her words, for a shorter duration, more a reflection; changing. Her face seems made to express, to have been given a new facility; seems helplessly manipulated. Witness of what the whole organism is undergoing, put to the test, to different tests, at different levels, by different organs of the body in succession.

A face in difficulty, suffering something, being worked from within. Words nonetheless peaceful continue to issue from it: Discordances, now slight, now very extraordinary.
When I gently remark on it she is most surprised. She is unaware! She is not conscious of being under siege.

qu'elle est assiégée.

Cependant l'ébranlement de son visage continue, progressivement fatigué, étiré, creusé, chargé, puis reconquis, puis à nouveau éteint, désuni, déplacé, disloqué, ayant perdu sa symétrie, enfin dégagé, éclairé, non sans être passé curieusement par plusieurs âges et par des transformations inattendues, indiscrètes, qui se découvrent sans façon, à quoi j'aimerais réfléchir. Mais le tout est trop rapide et divers.

En peu de temps elle montra une étonnante famille de visages, qu'elle portait sans le savoir, outre l'ancestrale, et celle de parents (éloignés ou proches), une famille potentielle, à l'évolution inconnue, que personne sans doute ne lui vit jusque-là; aux caractères multiples qui dans sa vie resteront susceptibles d'apparaître l'un au détriment du suivant; lutte à qui dominera l'autre, voilà que par le fait d'organes et de glandes diversement atteints, ils sont, en raccourci, avec l'humeur corrélative montrés en quelques minutes, dégagés, étalés, qu'elle ne voit et ne soupçonne pas et continue d'exposer, innocente.

Pour des physionomies différentes, elle dispose, je vois, d'une bonne douzaine sinon d'une vingtaine de figures incidentes, ou dois-je dire de cœurs, ou d'humeurs.

Étrange révélation, dont je ne ferai sans doute jamais rien, dont elle non plus ne cherche à rien tirer, ne consultant même pas, comme tant d'autres femmes dans son cas le feraient, un miroir pour connaître et apprécier ses nouveaux traits, son nouvel aspect et... aviser.

Je ne dis rien et laisse sans commentaires cet incroyable jeu de masques qui continue, souple sans but, sans utilisation et sans rapports.

Cependant mon cœur en chair et en muscles dans ma poitrine me fait souffrir, entretenant maux, malaises et pensées de désagrément.

Percevant ma difficulté, on m'apprêta avec des coussins la chaise longue face au jardin, permettant une meilleure position, d'où résulte un début de soulagement.

Un certain obscur refus de me relâcher, et même de seulement

Her face meanwhile continues to be assailed: it looks fatigued, drawn, lined, burdened, then repossessed, then again extinguished, bereft of unity, displaced, dislocated, its symmetry all gone, but clearing at last, lit up, and having passed in a strange way through several ages and through unexpected and indiscreet metamorphoses, quite candid exposures which I should like to dwell on. But it is all too rapid and various.

In a short space of time she displayed an astonishing family of faces, which she had borne unawares till then: her ancestral face, and the faces of her blood relations near and distant, and besides them a family *in potentia*, of unknown evolution, that doubtless had never been seen in her before, a multiplicity of traits which in her life will remain liable to appear one after the other and each to the detriment of the next, in a struggle for mastery. Now as different organs and glands are affected, they are shown in abbreviated form, each with its appropriate mood, in the space of a few minutes, detached and displayed, unseen by her and unsuspected, and she goes on exposing them, innocently.

For her different physiognomies she has, I observe, at least a dozen and perhaps a score of incidental aspects or should I say hearts or humours at her disposal.

A strange revelation, which doubtless I shall never make anything of, and nor does she herself seek to exploit it, not even – as very many women in her situation would – looking in a mirror to learn and to appraise her novel features, her novel looks and... point them out.

I say nothing, and I offer no commentary on this incredible play of masks: fluently it proceeds, without point, without use, without connections.

Meanwhile the heart of flesh and muscle in my chest is causing me some discomfort: pains, malaises, disagreeable thoughts.

My hosts, seeing my trouble, set out the chaise longue for me, with cushions, facing the garden, and there I am better placed and as a consequence begin to feel some relief.

An obscure refusal to let myself go, or even to try to, had

l'essayer, avait probablement sinon déterminé, du moins augmenté mon mal et empêché une accalmie.

Un disque. Un lied fut mis, puis écarté. Je ne voulais pas d'un entraînement européen et de cette époque.

Un autre disque, de musique Karnatique lui succéda. Les premières notes, à l'instant d'une importance inouïe furent comme frappées à l'intérieur de l'oreille même. Musique telle qu'on n'en avait jamais de la vie entendu d'aussi près. Elle nous cueillait au passage. Force intérieure de l'Inde, encore intensifiée; celle-ci apportait pré-éminence, poussait à la grandeur, alliée à de la ferveur, à une ferveur impersonnelle.

Comme l'eau avance dans le lit d'un fleuve, pareillement la musique avançait dans le lit de mon être, entretenant, entraînant ampleur, et aspiration à l'ampleur.
Mon mal avait disparu et l'appréhension.
C'était oublié.
Par des brisements de toutes sortes, et surtout d'une étrange sorte, la musique élue avait tout recouvert de sa façon unique.

. . . .

puis se trouva perdue en moi, perdue en tant qu'indépendante parmi une mer plus vaste.

Et le jardin fut présent, tout autrement présent.
Depuis le début une profondeur subtile avait gagné son extrémité. Il s'agissait à présent d'une toute autre chose, et même d'un tout autre jardin.

La musique sans plus ressortir s'était unie à lui, d'une union dont je n'avais aucune idée, si intime que je l'oubliais, union particulièrement forte avec l'arbre dominant qui s'y trouvait, à la double couronne très feuillue, agitée, agitée, sans arrêt, en mouvements inégaux, embrassés par une brise devenue «passionnée», ensemble inouï.

En des centaines de rameaux et de feuilles passaient et comme paissaient des aspirations insensées – que les sons d'une invisible «vina» rendaient merveilleusement généreuses, naturelles, débordantes.

probably brought about or at least aggravated my discomfort and prevented me from becoming calm.

A record. A *Lied* was put on, then taken off again. I did not want to be given a European impetus, and certainly not one from that era.

Then came another record, this time of Carnatic music. The first notes, at once of unprecedented importance, were, as it seemed, struck within the ear itself. A music never before heard so close. It took us up as it passed. This was the inward power of India, further intensified; it brought with it pre-eminence, reached for grandeur, came also with fervour, with an impersonal fervour.

As water advances in the bed of a river, likewise the music advanced in the bed of my being, and with it came a tide of fullness, and the longing to be filled.

My discomfort had gone and with it the apprehension.
It was forgotten.
Breaking in all ways, above all breaking strangely, the chosen music had covered over everything, uniquely.

. . . .

and then was lost in me, lost as a separate thing, in a larger ocean.

And the garden was present, quite differently present.
From the start there had been a subtle deepening of its farthest reaches. Now we were dealing with something quite different, even with a quite different garden.

The music had joined with it, and would remain there, in a union that surpassed my understanding, so close I was forgetting it, and the union was particularly strong with the largest tree in the garden, which had a double crown, very leafy, being shaken, shaken ceaselessly, in unequal shocks, and a breeze, becoming "passionate", caressed the tree, and their oneness astounded me.

Through hundreds of branches and leaves a delirious breathing passed or one might say it pastured there, and the sounds of an invisible "vina" filled it to overflowing with a marvellous richness and naturalness.

Sans caractère comme sans style lorsqu'en entrant et passant devant, je le vis si peu prometteur, le jardin quelconque se trouva alors d'emblée mué, devenu jardin paradisiaque... et moi devant à quelques pas, et si naturellement que je ne savais plus depuis combien de temps j'y étais, au Jardin des Jardins, celui où l'on ne songe à rien de plus, qui vous comble et par aucune chose au monde, même pas par du temps ne peut être dépassé, un vrai jardin de paradis.

C'était donc possible, et pas de pomme, ni de serpent ni de Dieu punisseur, seulement l'inespéré paradis. Et sans avoir à bouger, devant l'arbre même qui en était le centre, à la vaste couronne, aux jaunissantes feuilles charnues, annonciatrices dorées du proche automne.

Une brise s'était élevée, réveillant les rameaux endormis et les feuilles languissantes à l'ampleur souveraine, exprimant félicité, félicité au plus haut degré, et désir, désir de plus de félicité, félicités de toutes sortes offertes et l'instant d'après arrachées, reconquises, reconquises, réoffertes pour le partage et pour l'hommage, pour le don éperdu.

Le monde exalté de l'Orient était là, un et total, exprimant le summum d'extase au nom de tous, de tous sur Terre.

Ce que rameaux et feuilles peuvent figurer, aucun bras comme aucun corps de femme ou d'homme, aucune danse humaine ou animale n'aurait pu le réaliser. C'était des débordements, des débordements à n'en plus finir, élastiques et en tous sens, avec des nonchalances suivies de reprises inattendues, dans l'instant déchaînées, indépassables.

Agenouillements, supplications, enlacements, désenlacements, arrachages, plongées en avant, retraits, reculs, réembrassements et toujours à l'extrême, en chaque feuille, en chaque rameau, devenu être adorant, faisant et refaisant de profondes génuflexions, expression d'un infini hommage rendu, que depuis longtemps on eût dit que chaque fragment, devenu un tout, voulait rendre enfin sans retenue comme sans épuisement... et en hauteur.

Car ces débordements passionnés avaient lieu au sommet d'un arbre (et je ne m'en étonnais pas), sur un vieux noyer, à la cour-

Without special character or style, seeming to me so unpromising when I entered it or passed by, that ordinary garden now had in an instant sloughed off its outer appearance and become a paradise garden... and I was facing it, only a step or two away, and so naturally that I could not say how long I had been there, in the Garden of Gardens, where thoughts of anything besides all cease and you are filled and nothing on earth, not even time, can exceed it, a true garden of paradise.

Thus it was possible, and there was no apple, no serpent, no God of punishment, but only the unhoped for paradise. And without having to move, facing the tree itself which was the centre, the tree with the vast crown and its fleshy leaves already turning and announcing the imminent autumn in their gold.

A breeze had got up, and woke the sleeping branches and the drowsy leaves into a sovereign fullness, and showed forth happiness, the highest degree of happiness, and desire, the desire for more happiness, all kinds of happiness offered and a moment later withdrawn, then achieved again, achieved, and offered again to be shared, and to serve as praise and to be donated wildly.

The lifted up world of the Orient was there, one and whole, and in it the *summum* of ecstasy was manifest in the name of all, of all on earth.

Never will the arms and the bodies of women and men and human dance and the dancing of animals express what was there expressed by branches and leaves. It was an overflowing, an endless overflowing, fluent in all directions, with moments of ease and pause and sudden resumptions following them that became an instant breaking loose and reaching to the limits.

Kneeling, supplications, an embracing, a letting loose, a tearing up and headlong plunging forward and back again, back, embracing again and always at the limit, in every leaf, in every branch and twig, transformed into worshippers, again and again going down, deep down, to kneel, infinite homage was rendered there, as though every little part, become a whole, had longed to render homage without restraint at last and without exhaustion... and to the heights.

For this impassioned overflowing was happening in a treetop

onne large, si rare en cette essence, couronne double presque triple, quasi sans exemple, troupe dont chaque membre, infatigablement excessif, se précipitait en avant, se retirait, se reprécipitait sans repos.

Exaspération sans personne, où toutes les parties, branches, feuilles et rameaux étaient des personnes et plus que des personnes, plus profondément remuées, plus bouleversées, bouleversantes.

Individuellement, non communautairement, dans un rythme accéléré, emportant tout relâchement, où le vent réel ne paraissait pas pourtant le principal.

Feuillage s'inclinant bas, rapidement, puis fougueusement remontant, puis ramené en arrière, puis repartant inlassable, pour l'inlassable dépassement, froissé, défroissé presque sauvagement, cependant en vertu d'une sorte de consécration, avec une grandeur unique.

Beauté des palpitations au jardin des transformations.
Assouvissements et inassouvissements partaient de l'arbre aux ravissements.
Appels aux assoiffés, appels enfin entendus, exaucés. Le supplément attendu depuis toujours était reçu, était livré.
L'infini chiffonnage – déchiffonnage trouvait sa rencontre.

Et s'ouvrait, se refermait le désir infini, pulsation qui ne faiblissait pas.
Entre Terre et Cieux – félicité dépassée – une sauvagerie inconnue renvoyait à une délectation par-dessus toute délectation, à la transgression au plus haut comme au plus intérieur, là où l'indicible reste secret, sacré.

S'y ajoutait seulement, s'y agglutinait (venant on ne sait d'où) scansion imperturbable, un rythme sourd, fort, mais également intérieur, tel le martèlement d'un cœur, qui aurait été musical, un cœur venu aux arbres, qu'on ne leur connaissait pas, qu'ils nous avaient caché, issu d'un grand cœur végétal (on eût dit planétaire), cœur participant à tout, retrouvé, enfin perçu, audible aux possédés de l'émotion souveraine, celle qui tout accompagne, qui emporte l'Univers.

(which caused me no surprise), in an old walnut tree, with a broad crown, very rare in this species, a double almost triple crown, unique perhaps, making a troupe whose every member went tirelessly to extremes and flung forward and withdrew and flung forward again and never rested.

A ruffling of mood, and nobody there, but all the parts, branches and leaves and twigs, were human and more than human, more deeply agitated, more shaken and shaking.

Individually, not in a concert, in a hastened rhythm, overriding any wish to let up, and the real wind seemed not to be what mattered most.

Foliage bowing low, rapidly, then furiously lifting up, and then swept back, and starting again without fatigue, to go beyond and never be fatigued, ruffled, rubbed up almost savagely and yet as a sort of consecration, with a dignity all its own.

The beauty of things palpitating in the garden of transformations.
Assuaged and unassuaged by the tree of raptures.
Calling to the thirsty, calls finally heard and answered. Payment over the odds, waited for since the beginning, was received, was given.
Eternal ruffling and eternal smoothing here conjoined.

And infinite desire, a pulse never weakening, opened and closed.
Between earth and the heavens – beyond all happiness – out of a wildness never known before there came the old delight beyond all delights and entry was given, forbiddenly, into the highest and into the innermost place, where things that cannot be said remain secret and sacred.

To it was joined, with it was used (coming from who knows where) only a metre, a calm measure, a strong dull rhythm, likewise within, like the hammering of a heart, almost musical, a heart come into the trees, that we did not know they had, that they had hidden from us, sprung from the large heart of the vegetable world (from the whole planet's heart, as it seemed), a heart participating in everything, now found, now at last perceived, audible to those possessed of the sovereign feeling that accompanies all things and bears off the Universe.

169

Postures

Positions

Posture privilégiée

Par-dessus le divers,
un lac
un lac envahit

Coupé des bruiteurs
congé donné aux agitateurs

Mystère d'une posture

Vertu qu'on ne connaissait pas
Un je ne sais quoi comme un tertre
a soulevé l'être

Sur le divan
bras et mains immobiles,
et les doigts croisés,
unis derrière la tête
un cercle s'est réalisé,

Y circule un flux
qui la place agrandit,
agrandit

Bénéfique, apaisant
rejetant le médiocre voisinage
assourdies les interruptions
UN INVISIBLE INDÉRÉGLABLE CERCLE
a pris place

aisé
privilégié
porteur de grâce

Magie naturelle d'une simple pose,
Mis au calme
l'esprit en quiétude laisse ailleurs les parleurs
les menteurs inscrits,
laisse s'étaler les naïfs transporteurs
des quotidiennes maximes sommaires de l'époque.
Ne sont plus entendues, les disputes

Position of privilege

Above diversity,
a lake
a lake invades

No more noises off
the agitators have all gone home

Mystery of a position

A virtue unknown till now
Something like a little hill
has raised up the self

On the couch
still arms and hands,
and the fingers interlocking,
united behind the head
a circle has formed,

Through it a circulation
enlarges the place,
enlarges

Doing good, quietening
rejecting the mediocre neighbourhood
the interruptions are muffled
AN INVISIBLE DEPENDABLE CIRCLE
is placed

at ease
privileged
bringer of grace

The natural magic of a simple posture,
Calmed
the tranquil spirit leaves the talkers
the registered liars
elsewhere and lets the witless fetchers and carriers
of the everyday summary sayings of the age
exhibit themselves.
The disputes are out of hearing

Hors de l'action
bras retirés de la circulation
aussi bien de l'attaque que de l'aide
retirés de la préparation à agir...

Comme tout simultanément s'est retiré!

Embruns légers des discours dispersés qui se perdent
...
Professorales voix; lointaine
leur assurance vaine
qui serait risible
n'était le corps qui au calme s'unit,
seulement unit
au grand calme est uni.

Sous la tête,
les bras interdits de mouvements,
interdits d'interventions

Dans la tête
quiétude, harmonie, extension
Au bout le corps repose

Rien ne bouge
Plus de battues dans les bois
Plus de clairières
Soustraction

Abstinence règne
... savoir se laisser déposséder

L'esprit n'est plus détourné;
n'est plus offert aux distractions
n'en rencontre plus l'envie
Bain sans eau

Des provinces sans fin du corps allongé
on est sans nouvelles

Par-dessus un immense fleuve,
un pont s'est établi

Outside the action
arms taken out of the round
of attack and assistance equally
taken out of preparing to act...

How everything simultaneously has withdrawn!

Light spray of speech dispersing and vanishing
...
Professorial voices; distant
their vain self-assurance
which would be laughable
were it not for the body uniting with stillness
only uniting
united with extensive stillness,

Behind the head,
arms forbidden to move,
forbidden to intervene

In the head
tranquillity, harmony, extension
At the limits the body reposes

Nothing moves
No more beating through the woods
No more clearings
Removal

Abstinence reigns
... knowing how to be dispossessed

The spirit no longer diverted;
no longer given up to distractions
nor encounters the wish for distraction
Bath without water

From the limitless provinces of the body stretching out
no news comes

Over an immense river,
a bridge has arisen

d'une seule arche l'enjambant,
d'une arche unique se perdant au loin.

Pont-Prière
(pourtant sans prier)
vaste nouveau domaine aux ruisselants passages

Dans le haut du corps
quel enrichissement!

Celui-ci restitué, régnant, immortel
sa vraie grandeur retrouvée
sa noblesse unique
et prêt à plus d'ennoblissement
prêt à retrouver ailleurs
une supérieure Grandeur
incomparable, innommable,
le besoin en est venu
besoin d'une dimension extrême,
et qui s'imposera, qui régnera, s'étendra
Quel accomplissement!

Pont de l'infini,
on y est engagé

Renouvellement
de l'essentiel
du primaire essentiel
nu, et qui ne se démet plus
qui ne se laissera plus défaire
... là où soumission et insoumission s'égalisent

Plus d'éparpillement

L'avide guêpe
le dard oublié et ses vols, ses fols envols,
en son nid alvéolé se calme, s'est calmée

L'inutile éliminé

Abstinence a fait table rase
de ce qui à tort était aliment

strides it with a single arch,
one and only arch going into the distance.

Prayer Bridge
(and yet without praying)
a vast new country streaming with ways

In the upper body
such an enrichment!

The body restored, sovereign, immortal
back in its proper grandeur
its unique nobility
and ready for more ennobling
ready to recover elsewhere
a superior Grandeur
incomparable, unnameable,
the need for it has come
the need for a furthest dimension,
which will impose itself and rule and extend
What a thing achieved!

Bridge of the infinite,
we have entered upon it

Renewal
of the essential
of the first essential
naked, and it will never quit
and will not suffer itself again to be undone
... where submission and resistance are equalled

No more dispersal.

The avid wasp
forgets its sting and its flights, its escapades,
in its honeycombed nest it quietens, it is quiet

Elimination of useless things

Abstinence has cleared away
all that we fed on wrongly

en donnait l'habitude, la tentation
enterrant l'être
sous la masse du vain,
de l'inutile approvisionnement

Jeûne – vaste prolongation
... tandis que l'être aspire
aspire à davantage
davantage

Vacances sur place
Plus d'interceptions

... soustrait aux arrachements

Avec l'acquiescement, un complet acquiescement
le cœur repris, regagné
Comment l'avait-on ainsi perdu?
Le retrait enchanté devient l'épanouissement enchanté
Plus rien ne pourrait le suspendre.

Résurrection

Il y avait donc vraiment en soi une capitale!

Une grande communion à venir est là, attend, avance
approche
une communion qu'il sera impossible d'arrêter

sans angles,
acquiescement sans angles

dans la journée sans porte
espace
Rentrée en espace

and gave us the habit and the temptation
burying our being
under the mass of vanity,
of useless providing

Fast – immense prolongation
... and the self aspires
aspires more
towards more

Vacation here
No longer baulked

... removed from interruptions

Acquiescing, completely acquiescing
now the heart is regained and repossessed
How was it ever so lost?
The enchanted retreat becomes the enchanted florescence
Nothing could defer it now.

Resurrection

All along there was a capital in us!

A large communion to come is there, waiting, coming
closer
a communion it will be impossible to halt

without angles
acquiescence without angles

in the day without a door
space
Return to space

Posture II

étendu encore
étendu, mais cette fois tendu
le plus tendu possible

l'être comme en batterie
en son fond terré,
arc-bouté
en attente

Simultanément au fond d'un triangle
au plus profond de la pointe d'un triangle
allant s'amincissant.
en mouvement bientôt
en un mouvement accéléré

filant en arrière,
à toute allure dans l'espace qui le reçoit
l'absorbe
l'engloutit

soi,
être élastique
là en cette figure simplifiée
en conjonction avec une inouïe force balistique
inconnue, sans mesure, sans ralentissement

sans
arrêt

son expansion, son renforcement
à une vélocité toujours grandissante
en sorte que dans la confusion
des forces nouvellement apparues
il semble que, braqué, c'est lui qui fait tout partir
et se projeter
mais à reculons
à reculons toujours
À RECULONS prodigieusement

Position II

stretched out again
stretched out, but this time tensed
as tense as possible

the self as though emplaced
set in its depths,
braced
waiting

Simultaneously in the depths of a triangle
in the deepest part of the point of a triangle
thinning.
in motion before long
in accelerating motion

backwards
at full speed into space which receives it
absorbs
and swallows it

the self,
an elastic being
there in this simplified figure
in conjunction with a stupendous ballistic force
unknown, measureless, never slowing

never
stopping

its expansion, its being raised
to a speed forever increasing
so that in the confusion
of forces newly appeared
it seems, itself being fixed, itself to cause
everything to leave and be launched
but backwards
always backwards
astonishingly BACKWARDS

suite d'un simple angle
un coin de son insignifiante chambre
regardé fixément sans s'en détacher
... forme qui progressivement s'abstrait

Comme détaché de là
propulsé sans retenue
d'une détente toujours plus démesurée
hors de tout horizon bientôt
hors de tout
dans un espace
comme stellaire
toutefois sans étoiles apparentes
sans repères nulle part

en espace...
espaces

bolide
dont ne se perçoit pas le moteur
mais seulement l'entraînement à l'éloignement
à plus,
à de plus en plus d'éloignement

après des années, des décennies
en pensée tournant le dos à l'entourage

maintenant allié à cette nouvelle force étonnante sortie de faiblesse
mobilité comme magique entée sur l'immobilité du corps

non plus en aspirations, rêveries
mais devenu un être-engin matériel
et qui fonctionne
à sa place, sa vraie place
nullement absurde
transformé, réussissant

après tant de détours, enfin...

result of a simple angle
a corner of an ordinary room
fixedly stared at, the eyes unswerving,
... a form which more and more abstracts itself

As if detached from there
propelled without restraint
by an ever more extreme release
soon beyond any horizon
beyond everything
into a seemingly
stellar space
but without visible stars
without landmarks anywhere

in space...
spaces

a meteor
lost to what drives it
but only the drawing into the distance
further and further and further away

after years, after decades
in thought turning away from the surroundings

allied now to this new and astounding force born of weakness
a seemingly magical power of movement grafted on the unmoving
    body

no longer in aspirations and reveries
but become a material engine of being
that works
in its place, its real place
not at all absurd
transformed, succeeding

after so many detours, at last...

Posture III

Immobilité
Immobilité

étendu

à un autre niveau

autre niveau, autres accalmies

Plus d'enfantement
Comme une voile, le cœur «amené», contraint à se calmer

Corps comme une planche
détourné de toute complaisance

Jambes croisées
ou que lentement on décroisait
insidieuses variations de positions
qui à présent seraient gâcheuses, contraires

Les membres,
qu'avaient-ils donc si souvent à changer
à échanger?

détournements qui maintenant seraient ressentis
comme impostures

En la maison du corps-moi-émoi désormais annulé
leur souvenir méconnaissable va se dissipant

Éloignement
Retranchement

Au lieu des rapprochements, des insidieuses retrouvailles
une grand-place unie, lisse, s'est établie
à l'horizon ininterrompu

Nouvelle perpétuité.

Position III

Immobility
Immobility

stretched out

on another level

another level, other interludes of calm

No more giving birth
Like a sail, the heart "hauled in", obliged to be calm

Body like a plank
averted from all compliance

Legs crossed
or slowly being uncrossed
insidious changes of position
which would spoil things now, and be contrary

The limbs
why were they forever changing
and exchanging?

diversions which now would be felt
as impostures

In the house of the bodily self in commotion (henceforth annulled)
the dim memory of them is fading

Distancing
Curtailment

Instead of approaches, of insidious rediscoveries
a whole vast piazza, level, stretches
to the uninterrupted horizon

A new perpetuity.

Posture IV

Dans l'étroite salle
qui cesse d'être étroite
calme vient à notre rencontre
un calme de bienvenue
composé d'allonges, d'allonges
abandons non dénombrés

Emplacement n'est plus ici
n'est plus là
on a cessé d'en avoir, d'en vouloir

Du cotonneux en tous sens
vacillant, indéterminé
sur le passé qui sombre

Tourments, tournants dépassés
un corps pourtant non disparu a coulé

Lieux quittés
Temps du calme continu
parfait
non modulé.

Temps dans lequel on ne sera plus déconcerté
divisé,
dans lequel rien n'interpelle,
où ne débouche phénomène aucun

Plus de rencontre
Monde sans gradins
ou aux milliers d'imperceptibles gradins
accidents indistinctement coulissant dans de similaires accidents

Égalisation
enfin trouvée
enfin arrivée

qui ne sera plus interceptée.
On y vogue.

Jubilation à l'infini de la disparition des disparités

Position IV

In the narrow hall
which ceases to be narrow
calm comes to meet us
the calm of welcome
composed of extensions, extensions
innumerable surrenders

Placement no longer here
nor there
we have ceased to have one or want one

Cotton softness in all directions
wavering, indeterminate
on the foundering past

Torments, turnings gone by
a body, though not yet disappeared, has sunk

Places left
Times of lasting calm
perfect
not modulated.

A time in which we shall no longer be disconcerted
divided,
in which nothing intervenes,
and where not one phenomenon enters

No meetings now
A world without steps
or with thousands of imperceptible steps
undulations sliding indistinctly into similar undulations

Equalisation
found at last
come at last

will never again be thwarted.
And there we sail.

Jubilation without end at the disappearance of disparities

Bloodaxe Contemporary French Poets

Series Editors: Timothy Mathews & Michael Worton

FRENCH-ENGLISH BILINGUAL EDITIONS

1: **Yves Bonnefoy:** *On the Motion and Immobility of Douve /
Du mouvement et de l'immobilité de Douve*
Trans. Galway Kinnell. Introduction: Timothy Mathews. £12

2: **René Char:** *The Dawn Breakers / Les Matinaux*
Trans. & intr. Michael Worton. £12

3: **Henri Michaux:** *Spaced, Displaced / Déplacements Dégagements*
Trans. David & Helen Constantine. Introduction: Peter Broome. £12

4: **Aimé Césaire:** *Notebook of a Return to My Native Land /
Cahier d'un retour au pays natal*
Trans. & intr. Mireille Rosello (with Annie Pritchard). £12

5: **Philippe Jaccottet:** *Under Clouded Skies / Beauregard
Pensées sous les nuages / Beauregard*
Trans. David Constantine & Mark Treharne.
Introduction: Mark Treharne. £12

6: **Paul Éluard:** *Unbroken Poetry II / Poésie ininterrompue II*
Trans. Gilbert Bowen. Introduction: Jill Lewis. £12

7: **André Frénaud:** *Rome the Sorceress / La Sorcière de Rome*
Trans. Keith Bosley. Introduction: Peter Broome. £8.95

8: **Gérard Macé:** *Wood Asleep / Bois dormant*
Trans. David Kelley. Introduction: Jean-Pierre Richard. £8.95

9: **Guillevic:** *Carnac*
Trans. John Montague. Introduction: Stephen Romer. £12

10: **Salah Stétié:** *Cold Water Shielded: Selected Poems*
Trans. & intr. Michael Bishop. £9.95

'Bloodaxe's Contemporary French Poets series could not have arrived at a more opportune time, and I cannot remember any translation initiative in the past thirty years that has been more ambitious or more coherently planned in its attempt to bring French poetry across the Channel and the Atlantic. Under the editorship of Timothy Mathews and Michael Worton, the series has a clear format and an even clearer sense of mission' – MALCOLM BOWIE, *TLS*

Printed in the USA
CPSIA information can be obtained
at www.ICGtesting.com
JSHW082207140824
68134JS00014B/471